"But you don't know my circumstances!"

Do you want to live your life above your circumstances? God wants you to—and He will give you the ability if you will just walk with Him.

"Oh," you say, "but you don't know my circumstances."

"I've made a lot of bad mistakes."

"There have been some broken relationships."

"My dad just died unexpectedly."

"I have cancer."

"Our house just burned."

Yes, any of those, or any of a myriad of other situations could easily be your lot in life. It might be simply that you've had a bad day at work or an argument with your teenager.

Whatever your circumstances are, God knows them. He loves you, and He will help you, if you walk with Him.

ENJOYING
YOUR
WALK
WITH
GOD

How to Live
Above Your
Everyday
Circumstances

STEVE DOUGLASS

Win...Build...Send...people for Christ

Enjoying Your Walk With God
© Steve Douglass
All rights reserved.

Copyright © 2004
Published by Life ConneXions
375 Hwy 74 South, Suite A
Peachtree City
Georgia 30269
USA
Tel: 1800-235-7255
Fax: 1800-514-7072

ISBN 1-56399-240-X

To Bill Bright

*The person who taught me
so much about enjoying
my walk with God*

CONTENTS

ACKNOWLEDGMENTS

Any book is the result of the efforts of many people in addition to the author. The following people played important roles in this book. To them I would like to say a special thank you.

To Judy Douglass for her encouragement, advice and willingness to be flexible to an author's schedule.

To Ken Sidey for his many hours of able, insightful editing.

To Vicki Sidey and Brenda Heusterberg for their tireless typing.

To Dan Benson, Jean Bryant and Karla Lenderink for their ideas and accurate final editing.

But the fruit of the Spirit is
love, joy, peace . . .
(Galatians 5:22)

•

Be joyful always . . .
(1Thessalonians 5:16)

•

Consider it all joy, my brethren,
when you encounter various trials . . .
(James 1:2)

•

Always offering prayer with joy . . .
(Philippians 1:4)

•

Rejoice in the Lord always;
again I will say, rejoice!
(Philippians 4:4)

"But I Thought the Christian Life Was Supposed to be Straight-Laced Sober and Sad."

F rustrated, I trudged slowly back to my dorm room. My first exam in graduate school was just over. I knew the subject, but I'd blown it! Turmoil surged into my heart.

As I sat down in my room, a phrase of Scripture came to my mind: "But the fruit of the Spirit is love, joy, peace . . . " (Galatians 5:22).

At that moment I had no joy or peace. A simple prayer went up: "God, I'm not asking for any favors on the exam; I'm just asking for peace."

In minutes, God met me at my point of need, and joy and peace flooded my heart.

For the first time it dawned on me in a practical way that God intended me to live above my circumstances, and that He would provide the power for me to do so!

Do you want to live your life above your circumstances? God wants you to—and He will give you the ability if you will just walk with Him.

"Oh," you say, "but you don't know my circumstances."

"I've really made some bad mistakes."

"There have been some broken relationships."

"My dad just died unexpectedly."

"I have cancer."

"Our house just burned."

Yes, any of those, or any of a myriad of other situations could easily be your lot in life. It might be simply that you've had a bad day at work or an argument with your teenager.

Whatever your circumstances are, God knows them. He loves you, and He will help you, if you walk with Him.

The sad thing is that most Christians don't think of their Christian faith as being of much practical help. They often view it as a bit theoretical or other-worldly, or as simply what they do on Sunday morning contrasted to what they do during the rest of the week.

What is even worse is that many Christians view their experience with "things of God" as boring, stale and dull—anything but vital and exciting, or a source of joy.

They picture God as looking down from His

heaven and asking, "Hey, are you having fun?" When they stammer y-yes, He shouts back, "Then cut it out!"

That is what I thought — that Christianity was mainly a list of "don'ts." To a high school student, that seemed dull and restrictive — certainly not fun. Prayer meetings, sermons, even church socials, just didn't seem to have any of the excitement of the kinds of activities I had become used to: sports, dates and lively discussions. Christianity seemed so "vanilla."

So when I went to college, I thought I'd try it my way. I set out to be a success in grades, sports, leadership and social life. By God's grace a certain measure of success was mine. But the excitement — the joy and the deep peace of life — was not there.

The summer after graduation I met a group of students back in my home town, Rockford, Illinois, who were different. Not weird, but so much better off! They had joy, and they said it was because they were filled up with God, walking with Him day by day.

That idea didn't fit my opinion of Christianity, but they were so authentic. They really enjoyed life.

One night that summer I was sitting up in bed, thinking. Finally I prayed, "God, I don't really understand this, but if you could give me the kind of relationship with You that those people have, I'd like that. Let me walk with You like they do; let me experience the kind of joy You have given them."

Well, I didn't float off the bed, or for that matter, feel anything dramatic.

Slowly but surely, though, my life began to change. It wasn't much later that I went on for my master's in business administration and then had that experience of blowing my exam.

When it really hit me that God wanted me to enjoy my walk with Him, it seemed so fresh and revolutionary. Why hadn't anyone told me this before?

Well, they had: some of my friends, a Sunday school teacher, a pastor and his wife, my mother. They had shown it; I just hadn't seen it or believed it.

Besides, if I had noticed, I'd have realized the Bible shouts out that God wants us to enjoy our walk with Him. The apostle John makes experiencing this joy one of the main purposes for which he wrote his first epistle:

> What we have seen and heard we proclaim to you also, that you also may have fellowship with us; and indeed our fellowship is with the Father, and with His Son Jesus Christ. And these things we write, so that our joy may be made complete (1 John 1:3,4).

Here, and in the following several verses, John links this joy with our fellowship with God. As we walk with Him, we experience the forgiveness of our sins, the friendship of other Christians and the power of His Spirit, which produces the fruit of joy in our lives.

The apostle Paul was experiencing joy in spite of the circumstances he faced when he wrote his letter to the Philippians. He was in jail—possibly in a Roman dungeon, and he was chained to one or two guards. To add insult to injury, some other Christian speakers were seeming to take his place in ministry.

Wouldn't you be discouraged or depressed if you were in Paul's position? Well, he wasn't; he was exhilarated. In Philippians 1:4 he says he prayed with joy. Paul knew how to enjoy his walk with God anywhere.

There are 130 uses of Greek words for *joy* in the New Testament. Maybe that's why the Reverend Assembly of the Divines at Westminster penned as the first sentence of the Westminster Confession: "Man's chief end is to glorify God and *enjoy Him forever*" (emphasis mine).

God wants us to enjoy our relationship with Him. Yes, there will be bad circumstances in this life; we aren't in heaven yet. But God can and will empower us to have joy despite them—if we walk with Him.

How can you walk with Him like that? That is the point of this book: to show you how.

It's not complicated. Actually, it's practical and relevant to where life hits us.

What you will read will illustrate how it really happens—how it really works—in practice, not just in theory.

Do you want to enjoy your walk with God? It starts by learning how to *talk* with Him . . .

Talk
With Your Father

G od seems so far away."

"Can I really have a *personal* relationship with God?"

"I feel like my prayers stop at the ceiling."

"Prayer meetings bore me."

These and other frustrations I've heard expressed tell me that prayer can be a negative experience for Christians.

For example, many Christians think of prayer meetings as dull, stale, tedious and unvaried. They remember gathering in a small room, sitting in a circle of folding chairs, and after a short Bible study, moving into what was described as a "season of prayer." They knew exactly what was going to happen next. Someone — the same person every time — would pray for "all the missionaries overseas." Not by name, mind you, but with that phrase. Another would ask God to "bless our church."

The prayers were not conversational or personal. The language included "Thee's" and "Thou's" and other words and phrases heard nowhere in normal conversation.

For some Christians, serious prayer seems to be better suited to the less active people. You know, there are the *do*-ers, and then there are the *pray*-ers.

Or prayer belongs to that special group of superspiritual people, the "prayer warriors." Praying is their thing; they specialize in it. So we let them exercise their spiritual gift and pray for all of us.

Yet God tells us in His Word that we are to "pray about everything" (Philippians 4:6) and to "pray without ceasing" (1 Thessalonians 5:17). Does that mean that we are stuck? That this seemingly unnatural and unproductive activity is just a bitter pill we must swallow as Christians?

I have good news for you: The answer is no! Although talking with God is a necessary part of our walk with Him, it definitely doesn't have to be a negative experience.

On the contrary, our sense of the presence of God with us should be acutely positive. It certainly was for David when he wrote Psalm 23:

> The LORD is my shepherd, I shall not be in want. He makes me lie down in green pastures, he leads me beside quiet waters, he res-

tores my soul. He guides me in paths of
righteousness for his name's sake. Even
though I walk through the valley of the shadow
of death, I will fear no evil, for you are with me;
your rod and your staff, they comfort me.

You prepare a table before me in the presence
of my enemies. You anoint my head with oil;
my cup overflows. Surely goodness and love
will follow me all the days of my life, and I will
dwell in the house of the LORD forever (NIV)

Well, how can the rest of us feel that good
about our daily walk and conversation with God? Two
basic concepts have totally altered my experience
with prayer. The first is *perspective* — seeing God as a
personality — my heavenly Father, to be exact. The
second is *practice* — talking with Him as I go, instead
of saving up my thoughts until later in the day or
week.

PERSPECTIVE: GOD IS OUR FATHER

God is our Father — not just an impersonal
"Source" or a distant relative. He loves us, and prayer
is a means of developing a personal relationship with
Him.

It is similar to the way we develop a personal
relationship with another human being through conversations.

Can you imagine, as a child, talking with your
earthly father only a few minutes on Sunday morn-
ings and Wednesday evenings? Or, every time you
talk to him, only thanking him for the food his salary
provided for you as his child? Sounds pretty ludi-
crous, doesn't it? Obviously, that relationship is not

going to grow very much, if at all.

Prayer is simply *talking* to God; it can be just as natural as talking to anyone else. If we view prayer as something different, as an activity, for example, it becomes an end in itself and can seem stale and unnatural. We can easily lose our motivation for it.

Look back on any dull-prayer-meeting experiences you may have had. Is that what happened? Was prayer just another activity, and a rather slow one at that?

Often, even the way we talk about prayer can tell us how we view it. Consider some of the statements I have heard:

"I'm not prayed up."

"My prayer life is out of balance."

"I need a time of prayer this morning."

Do we say the same about talking?

"I'm not talked up."

"My talk life is out of balance."

"I need a time of talk this morning."

Why would we never say those things? Because talking is a means to a relationship with other people, not an end in itself. It is communicating with a person. It is meaningful and fun, something we do all the time. So why approach prayer any differently?

I am a father. I have watched my children, played with them and talked to them. And I have seen how natural it is for them to talk to me. Let me share a few observations about father-child communication, from this father's point of view. It should shed some light on how God, our Father, looks at our talking with Him.

First, how do my children greet me? With enthusiasm! For example, when Debbie was about two years old she would greet me unabashedly. As soon as she saw me, she would flash me a big toothy grin and run all the way across the room to me. When she reached me, she would jump up and down with her arms extended until I picked her up and hugged her.

Compare that with Hebrews 10:18, 19 and 22:

> Now, when sins have once been forever forgiven and forgotten, there is no need to offer more sacrifices to get rid of them.

> And so, dear brothers, now we may walk right into the very Holy of Holies where God is, because of the blood of Jesus. . . Let us go right in, to God himself, with true hearts fully trusting him to receive us. (TLB)

God invites us to walk right into His presence and greet Him as children would.

My children don't have a moment's concern as to whether or not I will receive them when they come up to me. As Christians, forgiven of our offenses to God, we should have no fear either.

Second, how do my children respond when they need help?

From their early ages, both of my children have found creative ways to get into trouble. Let me give you an example.

When Debbie was about three, she loved to ride a particular rocking horse. The rocking horse was suspended from a frame with big springs. She would bounce up and down on that horse for, it seemed, hours on end. One day I was in my bedroom when I heard a desperate scream from Debbie's room: "Help! Help!"

I rushed into her room to see what in the world was happening. She had tried to dismount from her horse and the cuff on one leg of her jeans had caught on one of the springs on the far side of the frame. That leg was stuck and twisted, while the other leg dangled in the air, toes barely touching the floor. Debbie was sprawled across the horse, suspended between heaven and earth, trying wildly to reach something—anything—solid.

Now, Debbie didn't stop, analyze her situation, and try a few possible solutions of her own. She just screamed out to me—her dad—for help. I didn't have to train her to do that; she just knew. Both Debbie and her sister, Michelle, have learned to cry out in times of need. We can do the same with our heavenly Father in our times of need.

David did. Look at Psalm 142:1: "I cry aloud to the LORD; I lift up my voice to the LORD for mercy" (NIV).

Third, my children have learned to ask me for things.

Debbie walked into the kitchen one time with her hands in her pockets. She looked up at the cupboard where we keep candy, then looked over at me. She looked down at her pockets, then over at me again.

"Dad," she declared, "these jeans have pockets. These pockets *need* candy."

Just as my children feel free to ask me for things, so God intends for us to feel free to ask Him for things. Look at Luke 11:9-13:

> So I say to you: Ask and it will be given to you; seek and you will find; knock and the door will be opened to you. For everyone who asks receives; he who seeks finds; and to him who knocks, the door will be opened. Which of you fathers, if your son asks for a fish, will give him a snake instead? Or if he asks for an egg, will give him a scorpion? If you then, though you are evil, know how to give good gifts to your children, how much more will your Father in heaven give the Holy Spirit to those who ask him! (NIV).

Also, we see in Romans 8:26 that God even helps us ask:

> In the same way the Spirit also helps our weakness; for we do not know how to pray as we should, but the Spirit Himself intercedes for us with groanings too deep for words.

God invites us to ask him just as children would ask. He even gives us assistance in the person of the Holy Spirit to ask.

Certainly my children have never been the least bit shy about asking, and neither should we be. God is a loving, providing Father.

Fourth, children respond to a father's expression of love. For example, I came home from work one day and walked into the kitchen. Debbie was sitting on the floor, screaming in anguish over some "injustice" she had just suffered.

I walked over and reached down to try to comfort her, but she would have no part of it. She pulled away and cried even harder. So I went over and hugged my wife Judy.

In a moment, I heard Debbie's screams subside. Then, out of the corner of my eye, I could see her watching what was going on. Another moment, and a little smile cracked the gloom on her face. She got up, ran over to us, let Judy pick her up, and then reached over with her arm and pulled me close to her and Judy. So there we were, all three of us demonstrating our love for one another. Debbie couldn't resist love.

In 1 John 4:16-18*a* we find:

> And we have come to know and have believed the love which God has for us. God is love, and the one who abides in love abides in God, and God abides in him. By this, love is perfected with us, that we may have confidence in the day of judgment; because as He is, so also are we in this world. There is no fear in love.

APPLICATION OF THE "GOD IS OUR FATHER" PERSPECTIVE

Do you think of God as your heavenly Father? Do you really? Do you feel the freedom to approach Him on any matter? Without hesitation?

If so, why don't you take a moment right now to mention something to Him just as you would your earthly father? Greet Him, or perhaps cry out in an area of concern. Ask Him for something you really do need. Tell Him you love Him. Thank Him for loving you.

God is your Father. Realize that. Act like it. Pray like it.

* * *

Now, what about that second concept: the *moment-by-moment practice* of talking with God? The next chapter explains this. It is one of the most powerful keys to enjoying our walk with God.

Let Your
First Stop Be God

When we got our home computer, it included several games. One is Snack Attack, similar to the popular Pac-Man game. Unfortunately, we didn't have a joy stick to control the player's direction, so I had to use four keys on the keyboard to make it move.

Boy, was that tough! Translating what I saw on the screen—the need to go up and down, left and right—into taps on the keyboard with my fingers was an extremely unnatural process. When I first played, I crashed into walls, and I was gobbled up by electronic enemies countless times. The game frustrated me and I was tempted to put it aside and never play it again.

With a little practice, though, I have gotten

much better at it. Now I rarely miss. I turn the right way at the right time. My fingers move instinctively. Pressing the right keys has become natural for me and I don't even think about it. It's a challenge to see how much higher I can score each time I play.

So it is with some aspects of prayer – they seem unnatural at first, but they can become easy and effective with enough practice.

THE SECOND KEY

One such aspect is praying continuously. I have found that the second key to enjoyable, meaningful prayer is to pray without ceasing, making it a steady part of our conscious thinking.

The first key, you remember from the previous chapter, is to talk with God as our Father. Prayer is the means to a relationship and can be as natural as talking when viewed that way.

In this chapter we will learn about the second key: *praying continuously.* That's where our needs are – in the moments of the day – not necessarily in the sequestered circle of our friends one night per week. Continuous prayer keeps prayer fresh and related to our lives, as they unfold daily.

King David knew and practiced this. In Psalm 16:8 he wrote: "I have set the LORD continually before me; Because He is at my right hand, I will not be shaken."

The word in Hebrew which translates "continually" is *tamid,* and it means "without interruption." David kept his mind focused on God all the time. He communicated with and thought about God continually.

What was the outcome? Peace and joy. In verse 8 he says, "I will not be shaken," and in verse 9, "Therefore my heart is glad, and my glory rejoices."

Of course, more could be explained about David's walk with God, how he praised and worshiped God and how he trusted God, but one crucial component was the *continuity* of his prayer life.

Notice how often in the psalms David uses the word *continually* in describing a good relationship with God: Psalms 25:15; 34:1; 35:27; 40:16; 70:4.

The apostle Paul also discovered this concept. The book of Philippians was written from prison, as mentioned in chapter 1. He faced the constant uncertainty of being tried and sentenced to death. In that context, he penned the words of Philippians 4:4,6,7:

> Rejoice in the Lord always; again I will say rejoice! . . . Be anxious for nothing, but in everything by prayer and supplication with thanksgiving let your requests be made known to God. And the peace of God, which surpasses all comprehension, shall guard your hearts and your minds in Christ Jesus.

How often are we to rejoice according to this passage? Always. As if that isn't frequently enough, you should know that this is in the present tense in Greek, which has a little different meaning from what we have in English. It means to "be in the midst of" doing something. You have just been rejoicing, you are now rejoicing and you will probably still be rejoicing in the next few moments. There is a sense of continuity. Therefore, you could translate the verse, "always be in the midst of rejoicing."

What's more, verse 6 goes on to say that we should be praying about everything. In our prayers, we should be in the midst of thanking God and presenting our needs. These verbs are also in the present tense.

So to whom should we be in the midst of speaking at all times? God.

And what is the outcome? "The peace of God, which surpasses all comprehension."

We will look more carefully in the next chapter at how a walk with God displaces anxiety. For now, let's consider that constant prayer is a command of God as well as a key to a peaceful, joyful walk with Him.

HOW THIS WORKS

"Great!" you say, "but how can I pray so continuously? When do I get everything done? When would I sleep, eat or work?"

Good questions. Let's look at how Nehemiah did it on one occasion and see if we can pick up some practical principles.

In the first part of the book of Nehemiah, we find him in a bit of a bind. A little background helps you understand the dilemma he faced. Nehemiah was a cupbearer. It was a cupbearer's job to taste things before they were given to the king to consume. The purpose was to prevent the king from being poisoned.

If the cupbearer ever had an argument with the king, of course, that was a serious matter — a *very* serious matter. For a cupbearer even to have a sad or grim face in the presence of the king was punishable by death. After all, he might be plotting the assassination of the king.

Unfortunate for Nehemiah was the fact that he had heard some bad news. Jerusalem, his home town, was devastated. The wall had been broken down and the gates burned. The people there were in great distress and reproach.

This had been weighing on Nehemiah's mind since he first heard about it. He wept and worried about Jerusalem for days. He fasted and prayed to God.

Now, in that context he was called upon to serve wine to the king. Let's see what happened (Nehemiah 2:1-5):

> And it came about in the month Nisan, in the twentieth year of King Artaxerxes, that wine was before him, and I took up the wine and gave it to the king. Now I had not been sad in his presence. So the king said to me, "Why is your face sad though you are not sick? This is nothing but sadness of heart." Then I was very much afraid. And I said to the king, "Let the king live forever. Why should my face not be sad when the city, the place of my fathers' tombs, lies desolate and its gates have been consumed by fire?" Then the king said to me, "What would you request?" So I prayed to the God of heaven. And I said to the king, "If it please the king, and if your servant has found

favor before you, send me to Judah, to the city
of my fathers' tombs, that I may rebuild it."

In this passage, Nehemiah had a sad face in
the presence of the king. When the king asked him
what was wrong, Nehemiah realized his answer could
determine whether or not he would live. So, as he was
speaking, he was also praying to God. He didn't have
a lot of time, but certainly did need God to intervene.

Although our problems usually are not a matter of life and death, the principle and the opportunity are the same. There is always time for a
momentary prayer. David, Paul and Nehemiah found
they had time. And so do you and I.

Of course, we can always choose to go through
our problems without God's wisdom, power or peace,
but that sounds kind of stupid, doesn't it?

"Okay," you say, "but specifically, now, how
can I do that?"

Let's go back to the story of Nehemiah. Do you
recall that Nehemiah "prayed to the God of heaven"
and then spoke to the king? Pretty quick thinking,
and praying, by Nehemiah, don't you think? Almost
as if he were doing three things at once: (1) listening
to the king; (2) praying; and (3) thinking of what to
say. Actually, when you consider how quickly our
minds can work, it isn't impossible to do these three
things at once. Let me explain.

Even attentive people don't normally listen or
otherwise pay attention to one thing more than about
10 seconds at a time. Our minds work so fast that
most activities around us can't feed in enough infor-

mation to keep our brains fully engaged for longer than that. So about every 10 seconds we're shifting a little bit from whatever is in the foreground of our mind to something else.

Since our minds are going to drift anyway, why not "let our first stop be God"? That's what I try to do. What I mean by that is to have a running conversation with God on whatever is on my mind just then. That might be what I've just been thinking about or perhaps what I'm turning my attention to. In the spirit of Philippians 4, I rejoice concerning what I've heard or seen. Or I pray for and ask for wisdom on what I'm about ready to think about. Or I thank God.

This doesn't take long. It may only be a few words of thought. It is simple, honest, spontaneous and pertinent to what is going on at the time.

In that way I "set the LORD continuously before me." In that way I "pray to the God of heaven," and then I say something to my friend.

No, I don't do this perfectly, but I try not to let more than a few minutes pass before I again talk with God.

Sometimes it's helpful to have a reminder. My wedding ring helps me remember not only my wife, but also to ask myself, *How many minutes has it been since I talked with God?*

AN ASSIGNMENT FOR YOU

Let me give you an assignment. Even as you read on in this book, I'd like you to begin to practice "letting your first stop be God." As you go from one page to the next, use that as a reminder to pray about what you learned, thank God, ask God or rejoice. As people or things come to mind in the next few minutes, mention a prayer about them to God. Is there some special need that person has? Pray and ask God to meet that need.

As you begin to master this practice, your life will not be the same. As the loving heavenly Father becomes increasingly present in your thoughts and as you specifically communicate with Him about your concerns, you will no longer look at prayer as just an order from God. You will tend to look at it as an incredible privilege and benefit to you. You will begin to experience what could accurately be called a constant fellowship with God, not just an occasional visit, and you will begin to experience that great joy and peace that can come only from a walk with God.

A number of years ago I was having lunch with a friend of mine. When his wife came to the table with her tray of food, the only available seat was to my left. She sat there.

As I talked with my friend, I practiced "letting my first stop be God." Whenever my mind drifted, I talked to God. It was brief. I didn't bow my head, close my eyes or fold my hands. I just directed my thoughts to God for a moment and then returned mentally to the conversation with my friend.

I hardly noticed when his wife got up and returned with a styrofoam cup of hot water for tea. She set it on my side of her tray. The tea bag and stirrer were still in the cup. She suddenly turned to say something to me, and she tipped over the cup of hot water, dumping it entirely onto my leg. Not a drop splashed on her. (Life isn't always fair.)

What did I do? You would think that I'd have cried out in pain and jumped up, right? Wrong! I laughed.

"That's weird," you say.

True, that's weird.

"That's not natural," you add.

True—it's *super*natural.

You see, it was a long distance from the presence of God to my leg. My mind was elsewhere. My peace and joy were being supplied supernaturally. So it took a while for the pain from my leg to penetrate into my conscious thoughts.

In the words of the song, "The things of earth will grow strangely dim in the light of His glory and grace."

* * *

If you want to know more of how you can experience God's peace in spite of pressure and anxiety, don't miss the next chapter.

Worry
and a Walk Don't Mix

Who likes things to go wrong? I sure don't! It wasn't my plan to have the hot water spilled on my leg, but I have yet to meet the person whose life runs 100 percent according to plan. All the precautions in the world can't guarantee it.

So when unexpected problems occur, what do we do? Unfortunately, we usually let those difficulties produce a lot of anxiety within us. That robs us of our peace, and we no longer enjoy our walk with God.

What *can* we do about it? This chapter will explain how to displace our anxiety with a walk with God.

It will go one way or the other. Worry will displace the walk or vice versa, because worry and a walk

39

don't mix.

In Matthew 6:31-34, Jesus says:

Do not be anxious then, saying, "What shall
we eat?" or "What shall we drink?" or "With
what shall we clothe ourselves?" For all these
things the Gentiles eagerly seek; for your heavenly Father knows that you need all these
things. But seek first His kingdom and His
righteousness; and all these things shall be
added to you.

Therefore do not be anxious for tomorrow; for
tomorrow will care for itself. Each day has
enough trouble of its own.

The Greek word translated "be anxious" is
merimnao. It means to have distracting care or to
allow mental focus to be distracted or split.

In this passage Jesus is teaching the strong
linkage between our walk with God and our degree
of undue concern about our daily life. He says we
shouldn't be terribly distracted or anxious over food,
drink and clothing because God knows our needs. He
will provide for them if we will just focus on Him, His
kingdom and His righteousness.

But what do we often do? We take charge! We
control the situation as best we can. Unfortunately,
we start worrying when things don't go our way.
Then we try to take even more control. So the situation spirals downward until we are really upset or depressed.

How can we stop the downward spiral? Do we
just do nothing about problems? No, God expects us
to take some action. The difference lies in who is bear-

ing the load, God or us.

If we walk with Him and trust Him for our needs, they are His problems. If we ignore Him and trust ourselves, they are our problems. The choice is ours.

Frankly, God is a lot better at solving problems than you and I are. We can feel more at ease when we know He is working on them. Our constant sense of His presence and provision displace our tendency to "own" or be "eaten up" by our problems.

Let's look at three means of making this displacement work.

TIME

The first means is *time* — that is, how much time do we spend thinking about our problems versus concentrating on the Lord? Matthew 6:34, for example, tells us to spend no time today worrying about tomorrow's problems.

To dig into this a little deeper, though, let's look again at Philippians 4:4,6,7:

> Rejoice in the Lord always; again I will say, rejoice! . . . Be anxious for nothing, but in everything by prayer and supplication with thanksgiving let your requests be made known to God. And the peace of God, which surpasses all comprehension, shall guard your hearts and your minds in Christ Jesus.

You remember from chapter 3, Paul conveys to us in these verses God's command to talk with Him at all times. He even prescribes some ways to communicate: rejoicing, praying, asking and thanking.

This command is valid whether or not we are anxious about something. Yet the context of this passage and its apparent purpose relate specifically to circumstances of anxiety.

Let me explain. In Philippians 1:27, Paul introduces the importance of unity among Christians. An illustration of whether we are walking worthy of the gospel is whether we are of one spirit and mind and are striving toward a common goal, much as athletes would strive to score and win by working together.

In Philippians 2:1,2 he repeats the exhortation to be at one with other believers and then points out what it takes to accomplish that in verses 3 and 4:

> Do nothing from selfishness or empty conceit, but with humility of mind let each of you regard one another as more important than himself; do not merely look out for your own personal interests, but also for the interests of others.

From there through the rest of chapter 2 and some of chapter 3, Paul continues to include this theme of humbling ourselves for the benefit of others and for the sake of the gospel.

So it is no surprise in chapter 4, verses 2 and 3, that he is concerned about two Christians who are not at one with each another:

> I urge Euodia and I urge Syntyche to live in harmony in the Lord. Indeed, true comrade, I ask you also to help these women who have shared my struggle in the cause of the gospel, together with Clement also, and the rest of my

fellow workers, whose names are in the book of life.

Why would these two, who apparently were mature Christians, not be at one? Well, probably because they each were doing what we would do: allowing ourselves to be concerned that things would not work out the way we want. When other people don't go along, we fall out of harmony with them. That way we can continue to try to control things and make them happen our way.

When my daughter Debbie was about four, she had the following interaction with my wife:

DEBBIE: Mom, I'm sad!

JUDY: I'm sorry Debbie. What's wrong?

DEBBIE: I didn't get my way. Someone took my way away and I want them to bring it back.

Wouldn't you guess that was a little of what was going through Euodia's and Syntyche's minds?

So what did Paul say next? Did he tell them *how* to subject themselves to one another? No, instead he shared how to have peace of mind. That peace would displace the anxiety that motivated each of them to fight for her own way.

Don't miss this point. Paul is showing how incredibly powerful the principle of displacement is. It overcomes even a strong, natural, human tendency to be concerned about our rights.

If we spend time and mental focus rejoicing, praying, asking and thanking God, we cannot also easily spend time and focus worrying. Verse 6 makes the contrast clear: Instead of being anxious (*merim-nao* again), we are to be prayerful *in everything.*

If we do this, the incomprehensible peace of God guards our hearts and minds in Christ Jesus. The word *guard* in Greek is a military term picturing soldiers who stand at the city gate and control who goes in and out. What a graphic picture of what our walk with God does to worry—it locks it out of the "cities" of our minds and hearts.

In summary, as we "let our first stop be God," we spend much of our mental time and energy talking to God and we don't have as much time and energy to spend worrying.

TOPIC

The second means of making displacement work in our lives is *topic,* i.e., what we think about.

Paul goes on in Philippians 4:8 to say:

Finally, brethren, whatever is true, whatever is honorable, whatever is right, whatever is pure, whatever is lovely, whatever is of good repute, if there is any excellence and if anything worthy of praise, let your mind dwell on these things.

The focus here is more topic than time. Our minds should dwell mainly on positive, constructive things rather than negative, destructive things.

I saw an interesting example of what *not* to do several years ago. I was waiting to board a commuter plane to fly from Ontario, California, to Los Angeles. As my plane pulled up to the gate and its passengers began to disembark, I noticed one particular older woman. She was visibly angry about something. She approached a woman standing near me, who turned out to be her daughter. I couldn't help but overhear their conversation.

It seems that when the older woman got off of her American Airlines plane in Los Angeles she was led to believe that her Golden West commuter flight would depart from "just right around the corner." Golden West actually was between 150 and 200 yards from the front of the American Airlines terminal.

The older woman was upset over the fact that she had "been deceived." Yes, that was all, but to her it was extremely upsetting. Her mind must have dwelt on that for more than an hour. She had worked herself into quite a fury—which pretty well ruined her reunion with her daughter.

Just think of what else she could have been thinking about: her daughter and her family, what she would be doing on her visit, the grandchildren, etc. All of those would have stimulated peace and joy in her heart. Instead she stimulated anger and emotional pain.

The choice of thought topic was hers, but the consequences were inevitable and became costly for them both.

Our emotional and mental well-being is generally better if we look at the brighter side of a given situation. Sometimes it is even good to laugh at our predicaments.

The story is told of a young man in truck-driving school. At the end of his course of study, he went for his final exam. It wasn't a written exam. Instead, the examiners presented driving situations to him orally and asked him for a quick response as to what he would do.

This was the first one:

"You are driving a fully loaded rig down a steep, two-lane mountain road with a small shoulder and no fence. Your brakes go out, and as you round the next curve, you see another rig coming up the road toward you. It is being passed by a third rig (which, of course, is in your lane). They are not very far in front of you. What would you do?"

The young man was thoughtful for a few seconds then smiled. "I'd wake up LeRoy," he said.

"What?" his examiners exclaimed. "Who is Le-Roy? We never mentioned a LeRoy."

"No, I know that," said the young man. "but you see, LeRoy is my partner in the trucking business. He's from a small town, and he's never seen an accident like this one's gonna be!"

Now that is definitely looking at the "lovely," "worthy of praise" side of a situation.

Sometimes it is helpful to take a step back from some negative circumstance and try to see God's purpose in it. Paul did that in Philippians 1:12-20. Remember that he was in prison. But look at verse 12: "Now I want you to know, brethren, that my circumstances have turned out for the greater progress of the gospel."

He saw a "true" and "excellent" thing to let his mind dwell on: the greater progress of the gospel that had resulted from his imprisonment. In fact, in verses 12-20, all but one verse make some reference to this positive perspective.

So instead of dwelling on the many negatives associated with his situation, Paul chose to let his mind dwell on the positive. As a result he was able to pray with "joy" (Philippians 1:4) and to be "content" (Philippians 4:11).

"Well," you say, "what if I have sinned and feel guilty about it? That's a negative thought. Should I just forget it and think about more positive alternatives?"

Good question. The answer is no! If you have sinned, you need to confess it to God and turn from it. When you do that, a very "true," "right" and "lovely" thought will fill your mind: You are *forgiven*.

David had that joyful experience:

> When I kept silent about my sin, my body wasted away through my groaning all day long. For day and night Thy hand was heavy upon me; my vitality was drained away as with the fever heat of summer. I acknowledged my sin to Thee, and my iniquity I did not hide; I said, "I will confess my transgressions to the LORD"; and Thou didst forgive the guilt of my sin (Psalm 32:3-5).

Forgiveness of the *guilt* of sin. That's a delightful displacement, isn't it?

Bruce, a Stanford University teaching assistant, certainly thought so. He had been led to Christ by one of his students the day before I met him. We sat in a cafeteria booth going over what had happened to him in becoming a Christian.

I read Psalm 32:3-5 to him. He paused for a moment as the significance sank in. Then he pressed his fists against his chest and exhaled deeply as he exclaimed, "Oh! You mean I'm forgiven!"

Forgiven! Let your mind dwell on that.

TASK

Finally, let's look at another form of displacement which can help us worry less and enjoy our walk with God more. We have covered time and topic displacement; now let's look at *task* displacement.

One time my wife heard a piece of particularly bad news. She decided to bury her sorrows by baking a batch of chocolate chip cookies (my favorite kind). When I came home that night, the delicious aroma of the cookies filled the house. I asked for some, only to find out that Judy had further displaced the pain by eating the entire batch!

I suppose we have all had the experience of doing something to take our minds off of a concern.

Paul seems to be referring to a form of that in Philippians 4:9: "The things you have learned and received and heard and seen in me, practice these things; and the God of peace shall be with you."

The "things," no doubt, were spiritual truths that the Philippians learned from Paul, but the point is, he told them to do them, not just think about them.

The result? "The God of *peace* shall be with you."

The task displacement is especially effective as we start doing what God asks us to do. Then we not only get our minds off our concerns, but we also inherit some of the pleasure of God in our obeying Him.

In November 1980, a terrible fire descended from the mountains above where I live and work in San Bernardino, California. It was fanned by gusts of wind up to 90 miles per hour. More than 280 homes were destroyed near the edge of the city, including homes of eleven families with Campus Crusade. Power lines and the bridge to one part of the headquarters of our ministry were destroyed.

To say the least, a number of us experienced a great deal of anxiety as we contemplated the situation. We certainly did pray and seek to cast our cares on the Lord. But do you know what He seemed to use more than anything else to give me peace of mind? My getting busy with helping to solve the problems.

We set up an emergency control center in one of the remaining parts of our headquarters. We lined up emergency supplies and shelter for our homeless staff. We built a temporary bridge. We restored the phone lines and other communication facilities and did many other things.

Our anxieties were displaced by the activities God led us into.

DISPLACE SOME OF
<u>YOUR</u> ANXIETIES

Well, how about you? Do you have any anxieties plaguing you? You would be a rare person if you didn't have some concerns.

Why don't you start letting your first stop be God right now as your mind moves from thought to thought?

Why not think some true, honorable, right, pure, lovely, good-repute, excellent, worthy-of-praise thoughts? They may totally displace some of the negative thoughts you are now having.

Is there anything you can do that would so immerse you in good activities that your concerns would fade?

"All right," you say, "I'm developing a healthy view of God as my Father; I'm beginning to pray without ceasing; and I've decided to find a way to displace some of my anxieties. Is there anything else?"

Yes. How would you like to *prevent* some of your problems? Sound interesting? Then turn to the next chapter.

Let the Bible
Keep You Out of Trouble

I have some goals in my life I'd like to achieve," the young woman in my office said. "I want to make the most of myself, and I'd like your help."

Because I teach management, I often get requests like that, and I'm always glad to help. But Sally (not her real name) had some difficult challenges.

As we talked, I learned that Sally had an eight-year-old child, who had been born out of wedlock. She was a Christian at the time the child was conceived, but, obviously, her walk with the Lord had not been all it should have been.

In fact, I began to see a pattern emerging in her life story. In that relationship, and in other areas of her life such as education and career goals, Sally had chosen to ignore what the Bible says and had made decisions based on what she thought was right at the time. I would explain what the Bible said, for example, about relationships or purpose in life, and she would respond, "Yes, but *I* have goals."

It quickly became obvious that her goals were not God's goals for her life, and though Sally said she wanted to walk with God, her own opinions were more important to her than God's.

A few months later, Sally left town. More than a year after that, I heard from her. She had moved to another city, where she had met another man. She again became pregnant. This fellow then married her, but divorced her after only five months.

I was disappointed, but not surprised. We had discussed what the Bible said specifically about sexual relationships. God's Word makes it clear. The place for sex is within marriage. But again, she had chosen to disregard what the Bible says. "I know, BUT . . . "

Now she was left with the burden of rearing two children without either father. That is a problem. That could well take some enjoyment out of life. Could it have been prevented? Yes, by obeying God's Word.

You see, the Bible can keep us out of a lot of trouble. Obeying its commands will result in our enjoying our walk with God much more.

"Well," you say, "that may be easy for you but I never found the Bible easy to understand or apply to my life. It seems dry to me—sort of like a textbook. And I was glad to stop studying textbooks years ago."

Join the club! That is how I, too, used to view the Bible — as dry, uninteresting and unrelated to my life. I discovered, though, how wrong I was. I now see it as my friend — a crucial ingredient in enjoying my walk with God.

Most Christians I talk to struggle with having a quiet time. Either they don't get to it or it seems a bit stale. I think the problem stems from a wrong perspective of the Bible and from a lack of certain simple, helpful practices.

PERSPECTIVE

Some people do approach Scripture as a if it were a textbook, and it seems too academic to them for real, everyday life.

Others may approach the Bible as if it were a devotional vitamin. They've been told that swallowing a few verses a day is good for them, so they do it. A quick reading every morning and that's it.

Or maybe, after trying one or both of the above, they arrive at the most common approach of all: *no* approach. Tired of the textbook, and seeing no benefit from the devotional vitamin, they just stop bothering with the Bible at all.

The end result of all three is the same — elimination of the Bible from a person's everyday life. That is a major cause of failure in the Christian's walk, and it surely robs him of the joy of his relationship with God.

There has probably never been a time of more Christian activity and knowledge than today. Innumerable seminars, books, tapes and videos are offered on every topic imaginable, from Christian aerobics to the end times.

This vast amount of knowledge available, however, seems to make little real difference in many people's lives. Christians are often barely distinguishable from nonbelievers. Something is wrong — Jesus Christ changes lives. A Christian's life should be different. It should be better. It should be more enjoyable.

One significant cause of the problems Christians have is the distance at which they hold Scriptures from their personal lives. One of my favorite Bible teachers, Dr. Howard Hendricks, says, "The Bible was not given primarily to satisfy your curiosity, but to overhaul your life." If God's Word isn't overhauling your life, you're either ignoring it or mishandling it. In both cases, one of the results is no joy in your walk with God.

Some believers, like the woman I just told you about, choose to ignore the Bible. For all intents and purposes, it is just another book on the shelf.

Others view the Bible as only a "heavenly" guidebook, filled with news of the sweet bye and bye, but with little to say about the here and now.

How sad those views are, because the Bible is packed with beneficial advice for daily living. It is nothing less than *God's* guide for this life.

So one significant perspective we need to keep before us is that the Scriptures benefit us greatly. In fact, the Scriptures themselves describe some of the benefits of being studied and applied.

> The testimony of the LORD is sure, making
> wise the simple. The precepts of the LORD are
> right, rejoicing the heart; the commandment
> of the LORD is pure, enlightening the eyes
> (Psalm 19:7b,8).

> Thy word is a lamp to my feet, and a light to
> my path (Psalm 119:105).

> Thy commandments make me wiser than my
> enemies, for they are ever mine. I have more
> insight than all my teachers, for Thy testi-
> monies are my meditation. I understand more
> than the aged, because I have observed Thy
> precepts (Psalm 119:98-100).

> If you abide in My word, then you are truly dis-
> ciples of Mine; and you shall know the truth,
> and the truth shall make you free (John 8:31b,
> 32).

> All Scripture is inspired by God and profitable
> for teaching, for reproof, for correction, for
> training in righteousness; that the man of God
> may be adequate, equipped for every good
> work (2 Timothy 3:16,17).

As we study God's Word, we literally become
more aware of what truth is. We become more en-
lightened. We become wiser than people who do not
know and believe God's Word. We live better, hap-
pier, more fruitful lives. Our minds grow sharper and
more useful to us. And Scripture gives a point of cer-
tainty from which we can go forward; we don't have
to debate over what is "truth" — and that gives us
more peace and joy.

For example, some intelligent, well-meaning

persons say that pornography does not hurt people and will not cause them to be more prone to the type of sexual behavior portrayed in the pornographic literature and films. It's not difficult to understand why they want to think that is true. After all, they reason, surely mature adults can control their behavior and can view these kinds of materials and keep them in perspective.

It sounds good, but it doesn't ring true to the teachings of the Word of God. Proverbs 23:7 tells us that we are what we think about. In Romans 12:2 Paul explains that we dare not conform ourselves to the ways of the world. Our very transformation into the kind of person God wants us to be depends crucially on the renewing of our minds.

According to the Scriptures, our thought life leads eventually to our action life. Christians don't need to wonder about that; they can know it.

Still not convinced of the Bible's practicality for daily life? Let's go a step further. Let's look, for example, at marriage. Do you think the Bible has anything to say about our building a strong marriage relationship? What do you think would happen to a marriage if the husband and wife really implemented the simple words of 1 John 3:23: "love one another"?

When Judy and I were first married, Judy's dog Loki found that I woke up more easily in the early morning hours than Judy did. So, if he wanted out then because he hadn't taken care of things earlier, he would come to my side of the bed and tug at my covers rather than Judy's.

I remember vividly one 3 A.M. trudge to the door when I asked myself why was I waking up to take this dog out when Judy was the one who had brought the dog into the marriage. This was her dog; this should be her job. I was never too keen on the dog in the first place.

But I'd been studying 1 John 3:23 and I realized it wasn't very loving for me to wake her up and send her shuffling through the house. The loving thing to do was to bear with this inconvenience.

God's Word had something to say about letting the dog out at 3 A.M. Now that's real life.

Need wisdom for raising your children?

Facing pressure on the job?

Do you need guidance on a career decision?

Strength? Cure for loneliness? Hope? Power for living life? Peace? Joy?

All of this and more is available through the Word of God.

With all those benefits, isn't it amazing that we don't spend more time in the Word? Well, that has to do with another key perspective.

Reading and studying the Bible, like prayer, can become an activity, rather than a means to a relationship with God. The Bible is not a textbook to be studied for answers which we spit out on a test paper. It is a means of communication from the Father to us, just as prayer is primarily communication from us to our Father.

Have you ever had a long distance romantic relationship? What is it like to receive a letter from your beloved? You just put that letter back in the mail stack and read the others first, right? Wrong! You drop the rest of the stack on the table, rip open the letter and eagerly read it. You study and meditate on many of the passages.

That is a little like the way we should view reading the Bible. It is a chance to drop whatever else we are doing or thinking about.

The Bible is a love letter from a Father to His children. Is that how you view it? A letter from a Father who loves you? If not, you're missing the life-changing joy that reading such a letter can bring.

The next time you contemplate studying the Bible, look at it as God's living, active communication to you. Think of all of the benefits the Bible gives you for living life. See what a difference these perspectives can make.

PRACTICE

Now let's move from perspective to practice.

Before people can apply Scripture and before it can overhaul their lives, they must understand it. One of the problems people often have in understanding the Bible is that they really don't know how to relate to it.

Many different Bible study methods can be used. But whatever method you use, to get the most from your time in the Bible, dig into the passage. Put yourself in the sandals of the people mentioned. Feel with them. Think with them. Picture the details. Live through the action. In other words, *relate* to it.

I'm not saying that the good old sit-down, dig-into-the-Greek kind of study of the Bible is wrong. I'm all for that if possible. Nor am I saying that a devotional reading of Scripture is wrong. Far from it.

All I am saying is that identifying with Scripture — feeling and thinking and reacting with God's Word — will help you get more out of your Bible study. It will turn your Bible study into a fascinating, exciting time. Why, I've even found it to be fun! Let me give you an example.

In Mark 2:14 we find the brief account of how Levi was called to be an apostle: "And as He [Jesus] passed by, He saw Levi the son of Alphaeus sitting in the tax office, and He said to him, 'Follow Me!' And he rose and followed Him."

When I read that short passage, several questions come to my mind. For instance, how do you explain a successful businessman like Levi (as the next verse implies) leaving his business because of just one phrase from Jesus? There is no documented previous conversation between them. What did Jesus do? Hypnotize him? "Levi-tate" him out of his office?

A little digging might help to explain what happened to Levi. First of all, recognize that tax collectors in those days were considerably unpopular, even more than the IRS is today. Tax collectors fraternized with Gentiles, which lost them the favor of the Jews. They worked for the hated Roman conquerors, and they collected taxes.

It became Levi's business, therefore, to know about other people's business so he could collect the proper amount of tax. As a result, he was probably a little nosey. I would venture to guess that his office was right out in the center of town. Not that Capernaum was that big, but I bet he was located where he could see everything going on. He might even have had informers to help him identify any tax cheaters.

For a minute or two, let's tune in with Levi. Let's think what Levi would have thought, feel what he would have felt. Picture yourself sitting in your tax office in the center of town, talking to people and collecting money. The sleeves of your robe are rolled up, a green eyeshade on your head, a note pad in hand. See if you can identify with the following conversation and thoughts by Levi.

Hey, step right up, step right up, come on in and pay your taxes. What's this? You say an itinerant preacher's been around? Jesus is his name? Very interesting, very interesting, just keep paying.

A voice from heaven at His baptism, you say! Turned water into wine at Cana? Well, that's not my district, but . . . I wonder if he paid tax on the production of that wine? Hmm. I've got to look into this man Jesus.

Hey, Simon. Come in here. I haven't seen you in a while. My records don't show any payment. How's your fishing business been? You haven't been fishing? You've been with Jesus? (This guy Jesus is going to ruin my business.)

Multitudes of people, really? Healing? Healing even a leper? No, no one's healed a leper. Simon, you can't fool me. I've got both feet on the ground.

You say He says the poor in spirit will inherit the Kingdom of God? Ha. Simon, I know that the rich in purse inherit the kingdom down here. You can't put that one over on me.

He said what to the Pharisees? Well, ha! I could probably agree with this Jesus on that point. Maybe I could even like this guy.

He says we shouldn't judge one another? Do you mean He teaches that people should accept even me? Really? Hm-m-m.

Plinius, the centurion! How are you this afternoon? So good to see you, sir. What's that? You say Jesus healed your servant? Meaning no disrespect, sir, but surely you don't believe the things this Jesus is said to have done. You're a rational Roman citizen, and . . . He really did it, huh? I'd like to meet this Jesus.

Hey, you! You, there. You look like . . . you are! You're Joseph, the cripple. What happened? How come you're able to be walking around? You say Jesus healed you? But, I've known you all your life. You . . . can't walk! You . . . He . . . ?

I'd like to meet this Jesus.

What? He's coming this way? Jesus is coming? Let me see if I can spot Him.

What? Who, me? You're talking to me, Jesus? You don't even know me. You don't know what I'm like, the things I've done.

You what? You do know me . . . and You want me to follow You? You bet I'll follow You.

Now can you understand why Levi may have responded the way he did? What makes the difference is rolling up your sleeves and getting into the scene with him. Doing this will take time and thought. You may have to use a few Bible study tools, such as a Bible handbook, an encyclopedia, a dictionary or a commentary, but the benefits are worth it. You will be planting God's Word in your heart. It will change your life.

To help you do this and to introduce a second practice, let me suggest four sentences to fill in as you study the Bible:

- If I were _____, I would have

  _____.

- This seems just like _____
  (a parallel in your own life).

- The best lesson I can learn from this is

  _____.

- This helps me know God better personally
  because _____.

For example, if you were Levi, what would you have done when Jesus asked you to follow Him? Would you have left your business behind? Or would you have questioned Jesus' intentions?

Perhaps, as you read this story, it will seem that this is the first time you have met Christ. Or maybe He is calling you to follow Him in a certain area of life but you don't know where that decision might take you.

What's the best lesson you can learn from Levi? Can you learn from his willingness to follow? Or perhaps you can learn that Jesus calls men and women from all stations of life, even yours.

How does this help you know God personally? What does it teach you about His character? His compassion? His challenge?

You see, with a little digging, a little thought, and the four simple questions, Scripture can become much more than a dry textbook or a spiritual pill.

Begin to use these four questions as you read and study the Bible. Do this with another passage, Mark 6:45-53, a story that I find sort of funny. The Bible? Funny? Sure! Life is full of funny moments, and the Bible is filled with life.

In summary, the first practice we learned was to *relate to* a Bible passage. Let me highlight the second practice. It is to *apply* the Bible to our lives. Now, it's one thing to relate to what the Bible says, but it is another thing altogether to apply it so it makes a difference in your life.

Make sure it gets into your life. Make sure you apply the lesson. If you do that on little lessons every day, through enough of a period of time, your life will change. People around you will notice the difference.

For example, some years ago Judy and I focused on teaching our younger daughter, Michelle, the

Golden Rule. In particular we taught her not to return unkindness for unkindness. Instead she was to be kind.

In the middle of that Debbie did something a little mean to her. Michelle didn't respond unkindly—she responded by being nice. Debbie said, "I didn't know what to do about it."

She knew that Michelle had responded in love. and that befuddled her. Ultimately, it caused her to be nicer to Michelle.

A third practice is to *meditate* as often as possible on Bible verses and their lessons. Consider the strong exhortation and benefits from Psalm 1:

> How blessed is the man who does not walk in the counsel of the wicked, nor stand in the path of sinners, nor sit in the seat of scoffers. But his delight is in the law of the LORD and in His law he meditates day and night. And he will be like a tree firmly planted by streams of water, which yields its fruit in its season, and its leaf does not wither; and in whatever he does, he prospers. The wicked are not so, but they are like chaff which the wind drives away. Therefore the wicked will not stand in judgment, nor sinners in the assembly of the righteous. For the LORD knows the way of the righteous, but the way of the wicked will perish.

This psalm contains both means and ends. The ends of the righteous are good and desirable. The ends of the wicked are undesirable to say the least—they will perish. The rewards of the righteous are detailed in verse 3. But what is the means? What must the righteous do? The answer is in verse 2. For the righteous man finds his delight "in the law of the LORD, and in His law he meditates day and night."

Let's substitute the word *Scriptures* for *law* here. When the psalms were written there wasn't as much of what we now call the Scriptures in place. The law was a main section of the recorded Word of God at that time. We now have more of His written Word.

If we delight ourselves in the Scriptures and if we meditate on them, we are thinking about them constantly day and night. Then the benefit—the prosperity of God—comes. God actually *may* bless you with earthly riches, but more important, He *will* bless you with loving relationships, an assurance that you are in the center of His will, and a deeper knowledge of Himself.

The difference between what the psalmist is talking about and our usual experience is continuity in God's Word, not just getting it in occasional spurts. I'm not against the spurts—like a quiet time in the morning. They're a good place to start. That is where you unearth things that can stay with you all day long, to ruminate on, as the word *meditate* means.

How can that happen in our lives? How can we implement Psalm 1:2 in a practical way in our lives?

One way I do that is to write Scriptures on 3" x 5" cards and set them in front of me—on my desk—throughout the day. Other ways include listening to cassette tape recordings of Scripture. Or I listen to Christian radio and TV. Or memorize Scripture. Or pray. Or listen to Christian music tapes.

As you do those things, the Word will displace anxiety just as you saw in the previous chapter. It will transform your life through the renewing of your mind. It qualifies you for God's blessing as you saw in Psalm 1. It keeps you out of a lot of trouble, and gives you blessing instead.

Recently I tried to assemble a pedal car for one of my daughters. The instructions were six pages long! But as I followed them, step by step, the car began to come together. In fact, the assembly was going so smoothly, I decided I had the hang of it and ventured a few steps on my own, without consulting the instructions. After all, I'd graduated with a degree in engineering. How could I go wrong?

Just as I snapped a locking washer into place — one that could not be removed — I glanced back at my instructions. "Do not attach washer until . . . " Well, I spent the next half hour trying to undo my mistake, and never did fully correct it.

Likewise, you can't afford to take your eyes off God's Word. Life is too complex. You need the Maker's instructions for living.

LET THE BIBLE
KEEP <u>YOU</u> OUT OF TROUBLE

Why not pause right now and ask God to help you relate to, apply and meditate on His Word better? If you do, you may avoid some terrible mistakes.

Learn to Like
What You Have to Do

Debbie, go clean up your room."

"I'll die. I'll just die if I have to clean up my room!"

"Go clean it up anyway."

"Hummph!"

Fifteen minutes later Debbie emerged from her room and my wife said, "Well, did you clean up your room?"

"Yes."

"Did you die?"

" . . . yes . . . and I came alive again!"

Do some things you have to do cause you to throw up your hands and say, "I'll die; I'll just die if I have to do that one more time"?

Most of us have at least a few of those kind of activities. For example, I don't like to make phone calls. Too bad that on any day my office desk may have as many as twenty or thirty message slips of calls I need to make.

Maybe you don't like doing household chores — dishes, cooking, laundry, ironing, taking out the trash or mowing the lawn. Or maybe it's filing, correspondence, sales calls, meetings or working out in the rain or heat. Or maybe relating to certain people drives you nuts.

Face it, there are lots of things we *have* to do. Unfortunately, those aren't always the things we *like* to do. These distasteful have-to-do activities I call "liver" activities.

One of the serious problems of having too many liver activities is that they easily can get us frustrated and angry. We tend to procrastinate and that makes us feel unproductive, and guilty as well. We then begin to worry about them more and more, and we get pretty discouraged with ourselves.

Frustration, anger, guilt, worry and discouragement aren't very enjoyable, are they? Too many liver activities can be huge blockages to enjoying a walk with God.

In an earlier chapter you learned some ways to *displace* worries as they occur. In this chapter you will learn ways to *prevent* some worries from occurring. You will learn how to like what you have to do.

I'm sure this sounds too good to be true. But consider the following story as an illustration of how it can happen:

A woman married a man who turned out to be demanding. Every day he would give her a list of things to do that day: wash the dishes, clean and dust the house, shop for groceries, wash and iron his clothes, tend the garden, prepare dinner.

When he returned home from work in the evening he would check to see that she had completed her assigned chores. If she failed to complete some of the tasks, he'd complain bitterly. "I work all day for us. Can't you even do these few things for our marriage . . . for our home?"

The woman was, frankly, miserable.

After years of marriage, the husband died, and in time, the woman remarried.

Her new husband was the opposite of her first. Kind and gentle, he never demanded a thing. Her life filled with joy as she basked in her new husband's love.

One day, as the woman was working in the kitchen, she happened across one of her first husband's list of chores. When she read it, she was surprised to realize that she was now doing even more housework than she had in her previous marriage—but the misery and drudgery were long gone. She was motivated from within, by love, to do what she had to do.

The real difference between doing something with joy or with drudgery (and who wants drudgery?) is whether or not we are internally motivated. No amount of external pressure can substitute for the genuine interest and zeal that is produced by internal motivation.

Just think of the things you do because you like to do them. How readily do you get to them? How few times do you procrastinate? How much more rapidly and pleasurably do you do them? Life is too short to be stuck with drudgery, and it's just a lot easier and more enjoyable to do what we like to do than what we don't like to do.

But woe to any necessary task for which we aren't motivated. We avoid it. We procrastinate. And when we don't do it, we feel guilty because we haven't done what we should have. Anxiety sets in. We grumble. We finally put in minimum effort, and then we get results of equal quality.

Distaste for any activity of life detracts from our walk with God through frustration, anger, etc., but distaste for activities which are an important part of our Christian walk is double jeopardy. We are not just frustrated; we also are procrastinating, and we do poorly in the very things that could make our walk with God closer and more enjoyable.

PERSPECTIVE

How do you currently feel about prayer? Bible study? Church attendance? Witnessing? Are they just a list of Christian "chores"? Or are they vital, exciting parts of your walk with God which you do as a response to His love?

In previous chapters we have thought together about gaining internal motivation for prayer and Bible study. Now let's look at the ways you can learn to enjoy those and other key Christian attitudes and actions. For that matter, you will learn ways to like to do anything you have to do.

Let's start with perspective. Do you think God wants you to experience joy in living your life? Well, He does. Look at what He says in His Word:

> Delight yourself in the LORD; And He will give you the desires of your heart. Commit your way to the LORD, trust also in Him, and He will do it (Psalm 37:4,5).

> But the Fruit of the Spirit is love, joy . . . (Galatians 5:22).

> Be joyful always (1 Thessalonians 5:16).

Apparently God intends for us to enjoy our Christian lives. Sure, there will be disappointments and trials. Yes, there will be challenging, hard-to-like activities. Still, without qualification, God tells us to "be joyful always."

Can this really happen? Consider a question I often ask Christian audiences to whom I speak: "How many of you enjoyed reading and studying the Bible before you became Christians?"

Very few people raise their hands. But then I ask, "How many of you *now* like to read the Bible?"

Many raise their hands. What's the difference? God has worked in their lives. He has caused many Christians to have new internal motivation concerning Bible study.

How does God do this? How does He change our desires? He does it through His Holy Spirit, a powerful motivator who dwells in every Christian. Did you notice in Galatians 5:22 that joy is part of the fruit of the Holy Spirit?

God has placed within us the ultimate source of internal motivation — His Spirit. In Ephesians 3:16 Paul prays that God would grant us "according to the riches of His glory, to be strengthened with power through His Spirit in the inner man."

The Holy Spirit is so important to our walk with God that I have dedicated an entire later chapter to His role. For now, though, it is sufficient to have the perspective that God can empower us to like what we have to do.

So God *wants us to enjoy* our walks with Him and He *gives us the power* to have joy. How, then, do we go about this business of enjoying our liver activities? Well, beyond keeping the right perspective, we practice to increase our internal motivation.

PRACTICE

First, *pray specifically that God will enable you to enjoy what you have to do.*

As we saw above, He can and will give you new desires. Philippians 2:13 says, "For it is God who is at work in you, both to will and to work for His good pleasure."

Do you think it's appropriate to ask God to give you joy to do something you must do? I believe it is.

Think right now of a regular activity that you really don't like. Perhaps it is washing dishes, typing long letters, keeping financial records, or driving long distances. Or maybe it is prayer, Bible study or witnessing.

Pray that God will change your desire and cause you to like it. Keep praying and thanking God that He will work in you to give you the will and desire to carry out your have-to activity.

It is demotivating not to know why you are doing something, so,

Second, *remind yourself why you are doing what you're doing.*

For example, why might a person want to lose weight? Reasons might include a more attractive appearance, better health, and a longer life.

An even better reminder is a graphic one. A picture is worth a thousand words, and it can provide a lot of motivation.

For example, I knew a woman who was trying to diet, but she was having great difficulty with it. So she decided to put on her refrigerator door a magazine picture of a very shapely model dressed in a scanty bikini.

Why did she do that? (It had an entirely different impact on me than it had on her!) She did it so that when she was tempted to snack and went to the refrigerator, she would see that shapely body and say, "If I don't eat now, I could begin to look like she does."

I've thought since that a good addition to her strategy would be to put a picture of a hippopotamus on the *inside* of the refrigerator door along with the statement: "Now that you are in here, this is what you are going to look like."

Third, *enlist the help of a friend.*

Do what you don't like with someone you *do* like. I knew a young man in college who was a terrible student—mainly because he never studied. He never opened his textbooks.

Then he met a good-looking young woman who was a very good student. Where do you suppose he could find her on a typical week night? That's right, at the library.

I can just imagine how he tried to impress her the first night he came to the library. His arms were loaded with textbooks (the ones he hadn't opened). Can you imagine the loud cracking of each book as he opened it for the first time? Not too impressive!

But after many months of spending time reading his books at the library, his grades began to improve. Why? Because he enlisted his girlfriend's help in becoming motivated to do what he had to do: study.

Fourth, *make a game out of your liver activity.*

That is how I remedied my dislike for phone calls. What was discouraging to me was that, after I had returned five or ten calls, my secretary would walk up with several more messages. I wasn't making any progress.

Finally an idea came to me. Every time I talked to someone, I would put a mark on a particular 3" x 5" card. After a number of phone conversations, the marks on the card served as tangible evidence of progress.

Then an improved idea came to me. If I was able to leave a message for the other person, I would also put a mark. That was all I could do if they weren't there, right?

Now the marks accumulated a good deal more rapidly. Then the ultimate improvement occurred to me. Every time I dialed the phone I would put a mark — whether I talked to the person, left a message or even got a wrong number!

"That's not fair," you say.

Well, it's my game! I can play it any way I want!

You make up yours, and you can play it any way you want!

Actually, my phone game also illustrates another way to increase your motivation for liver activities:

Fifth: *Keep the results in view.*

Ask yourself, "Where are the bowling pins here?" What do I mean by that?

Imagine a bowling alley where the pins were set behind strips of cloth or opaque plastic strips that would let the ball go through but would hide the pins from view. You might hear the sound of pins falling, but you wouldn't see how many you knocked down. How many people do you think would bowl?

Make sure you notice and keep within your view any progress you are making on that difficult assignment.

APPLY THIS NOW

You have just read about some perspectives and practices to help you enjoy your walk with God when you are confronted with a liver activity. If ever there is something you want to apply right away, this is it. Here it is in specific steps:

1. Think of some specific have-to activity you don't enjoy. If possible, think of one that relates directly to your Christian growth and walk, witnessing, for example.

2. Pray and ask God to give you a desire to do what you need to do.

3. Then review the other points in the chapter and apply one of them.

4. Put up some reminders as to why you are doing this particular thing. Can you do it with someone?

5. Note how quickly God works within you to cause you to like what you have to do.

See Adversity
as God's Opportunity

I remember as if they were yesterday the events of Good Friday, 1978. I'd gotten up to run, as was my habit. As I went out, I noticed my dad sitting up in his room at the other end of the house. He had been diagnosed as having cancer just one month before. He seemed to be slipping fast.

When I returned from my run, I didn't notice him sitting up, although the light was still on in his room. I went into my bathroom, took a shower and got dressed. On my way out to my prayer time at the chapel, I decided to stop and make sure Dad was up. I was to take him to the hospital for a radiation treatment in about an hour.

When I entered his room, I knew something was wrong. I don't know if it was a lack of motion in his chest or something else, but I knew he was dead.

Since I'd seen him so recently, I rushed over and sought to revive him with every technique I could think of. Then it was almost as if God pulled me back by the shoulders, wrapped His arms around me and gave me the assurance that this was His will.

By this time, as you might well imagine, people were running around, and there was a great deal of commotion. But God gave me peace, and it was almost as though someone had shut the door between me and the noise. I still could hear it, but it was a low sound in my ears.

Finding Dad dead was one of the major points of adversity in my entire life. I knew he was dying, but that still had not totally prepared me for this moment of his death. Now there was no longer any hope that things would be better. Something unchangeable had occurred; Dad was dead.

BEYOND DISPLACEMENT

There are some things you can't just "displace" from your thoughts as we discussed in a previous chapter. To cope with such major traumas, we are forced to take a big step beyond that, to deal with problems on a different, higher level.

The questions that inevitably will come to mind when we face these things are: Why? Why did this happen? Why did this happen to me?

I wish I had the answers to all those "why" questions in my life.

When there are no answers to those questions, we can lose heart. I know one person who had been successful financially. Then through circumstances beyond his control, he was forced to consider bankruptcy. As he approached the moment of decision to declare bankruptcy, I recall how he seemed to lose heart. He wouldn't even try to do certain things that could have helped save some of the financial empire that he had worked so hard to assemble. The circumstances had become too great for him to bear. It was easier to wash his hands and start anew.

Another response to the prospect of adversity is to try to avoid it completely. One man wanted to escape the turmoil of impending war in Europe in the 1930s. He fled with his family to a tiny island in the South Pacific. He figured he was as far away as he could get from the threat of battle. The island he fled to? Iwo Jima.

It is inevitable that some problems will arise. A loved one will eventually die. Serious illness, financial setback, family turmoil — any or all can strike unexpectedly. How can we experience joy in spite of them? Can we really enjoy a walk with God during tragedy?

After all, isn't it normal to become discouraged or depressed? But giving up, or living in constant fear, falls far short of the joy God intends us to have.

Our lives may not always be filled with happiness. We may hurt. We may mourn and grieve. Yet, if there is anything to a strong walk with God, those who follow Him and fellowship with Him should be able to go through life's inevitable bad circumstances without being utterly destroyed emotionally or becoming devoid of joy.

"Well," you say, "I'm sorry to hear that I am signed up for that course. But suppose I pass the final. Will I actually be a more useful, productive person?"

Good question. There is a particularly encouraging answer: Yes. Normally, God will open doors of opportunity to us *after* we have submitted ourselves to His plans for our growth.

The purpose of this chapter is to provide some perspective and practice to help you emerge from adversity as a stronger, more joyful person.

PERSPECTIVE

Perhaps the biggest reason we fail to find any strength or joy in adversity is that we lose sight of God's perspective. 1 Peter 4:12,13 and 5:10 begin to explain God's perspective:

> Beloved, do not be surprised at the fiery ordeal among you, which comes upon you for your testing, as though some strange thing were happening to you; but to the degree that you share the sufferings of Christ, keep on rejoicing, so that also at the revelation of His glory, you may rejoice with exaltation . . . And after you have suffered for a little while, the God of all grace, who called you to His eternal glory in Christ, will Himself perfect, confirm, strengthen and establish you.

The first thing we note in these passages is that we shouldn't be surprised when we go through ordeals. It would be nice to avoid them, but that isn't God's plan. After we have suffered for a little while, though, God will *use* them to perfect, to confirm, to strengthen, and to establish us.

James makes the same point in his letter:

Consider it all joy, my brethren, when you encounter various trials, knowing that the testing of your faith produces endurance. And let endurance have its perfect result, that you may be perfect and complete, lacking in nothing (James 1:2-4).

Particularly notice that phrase "perfect and complete, lacking in nothing." *Teleioi* is the Greek word here for "perfect" and it has the connotation of spiritually mature. The word *complete* in this context seems to mean having all the necessary elements of Christian virtue and character. "Lacking in nothing" simply reiterates that point.

It is with this wonderful outcome in mind that James says, "Consider it all joy, my brethren, when you encounter various trials." Trials inaugurate a process of growth and maturity in our character.

It is a little like training for sports. I played basketball all the way through college. My high school coach was Dolph Stanley—an outstanding coach, but I'll never forget the pain he put us through. Night after night he would have us run up and down the court practicing fast breaks for 30 minutes to an hour. I thought I would die from exhaustion.

When we competed against other teams, I began to understand why he did that. In the fourth quarter we still were going strong while the other teams were tired.

Late in the season in my senior year we played Chicago Carver. They were bigger and stronger than we were. They had beaten some outstanding teams. A few weeks later they went on to win the Illinois State Championship.

But on that particular night they met a team that was in good enough shape to run them into the ground. We beat them by 30 points as our fast break worked to perfection. Our earlier painful practices had brought us to a high point of physical capability.

Likewise God uses adversity to our long-term benefit. Adversity is intended to bring about "quality growth" in our lives. It's an instrument in God's hands to fashion us into the kind of people God wants us to be.

We tend to be far more concerned about circumstances than God is. We also tend to be far less concerned about character than God is. As a result, we would gladly accept better circumstances even though it might mean much less character growth in us. God will not settle for that. He insists that we grow to be strong oak trees, not weak sprigs.

So adversity leads to quality growth. Is that it? Are we just supposed to bask in our quality and character, much as a body builder might flex his muscles in front of a mirror?

HOW GOD PREPARES US
FOR OPPORTUNITIES

No, that's not it. God causes us to grow so that we are prepared for His special opportunities.

In Peter 5:6 we read: "Humble yourselves, therefore, under the mighty hand of God, that He may exalt you at the proper time."

Ephesians 2:10 says, "For we are His workmanship, created in Christ Jesus for good works, which God prepared beforehand, that we should walk in them."

Just as quality growth is intended to follow adversity, so a few other steps are to follow that quality growth. As we grow, we become prepared. In the Ephesians passage we see a picture of God as a craftsman. Picture Him chiseling some wood off here, filing and sanding some off there. Why? So that piece of wood can be prepared in beauty and be functional for future use.

Then comes the proper time — when God offers His perfect opportunity.

Let me give you an example. A number of years ago, through some unavoidable circumstances, I felt cut off from certain opportunities for evangelism. For some that might not be a problem, but it really disappointed me. I thought of it as a significant adversity. God used that, though, to cause me to pray and seek more personal preparation in the area of evangelism.

I grew in ways I wouldn't have otherwise. I began to experiment with different ways in which to reach people for Christ and discovered a film called "Football Fever." It is an excellent evangelistic, highly entertaining film. It has scenes from the National Football League games with bone-crunching tackles and outstanding catches and then a number of humorous plays where it seems like everybody touches the ball but no one can recover the fumble. Intermixed with all of these, bits and pieces of the lives of different men in the NFL who have been touched by Jesus Christ are presented.

In my Sunday school class, I had the opportunity to rent this film for two weeks. We heavily promoted the event, and on the first day of class, 156 people showed up. That was far more than our normal attendance. That morning, 12 people indicated decisions for Jesus Christ. That is exciting.

But, probably more exciting is the fact that 15 couples came to the front of the class afterward to arrange to show the film. They passed it from hand to hand—the equipment, the film, everything. They showed that film 28 times in two weeks, an average of twice a day. Approximately 1,500 people were exposed to the gospel. The next year, we did the same thing and about 2,000 people were exposed to the gospel.

I have found that if I submit to God's preparation, usually the "proper time" comes, that time which God has planned for me. It is His perfect opportunity, and sometimes that leads to productivity—or quantity growth—beyond my wildest imagination.

Let me continue with my evangelism illustration. Through the adversity, God continued to push me into finding some new ways of evangelizing. In June of 1983 He apparently thought I was prepared to be helpful on a bigger scale.

One day Bill Bright, the founder and president of Campus Crusade for Christ, called me into his office. Nancy DeMoss, the chairman of the board of the Arthur S. DeMoss Foundation, was on the phone. She explained that the DeMoss Foundation wanted to do a major media evangelistic campaign in association with The Year of the Bible efforts. She asked me to manage the campaign.

To pull off a huge nationwide media campaign successfully in seven months is impossible, as any advertising person will tell you. So God truly deserves all the credit for what occurred.

By the end of the campaign, about 7 million people had requested the evangelistic book *Power for Living* and an estimated 700,000 people had indicated decisions for Christ.

What an incredibly productive opportunity it was from the Lord!

GOD'S ADVERSITY PROCESS

My experience in evangelism in the last several years is but one illustration in my life of God's "adversity" process:

1. Adversity leads to quality growth.
2. Quality growth leads to preparedness.
3. Preparedness leads to opportunity.
4. Opportunity leads to quantity growth (productivity).

Look at Saul (who later became the apostle Paul). His life contains another example. He persecuted Christians until, on the road to Damascus, he was blinded by God. There Christ Himself called Saul to a ministry for Him.

For three days, Saul was blind. Wouldn't you suppose he grew a great deal in his thoughts and attitudes about Christ? Here he'd been totally opposed to Him and now, all of a sudden, he discovered that Jesus was the Lord of all. It must have been a time of real adjustment and growth. By the end of that time, God had Saul prepared and sent Ananias to see him.

Ananias was the instrument God used to heal Saul. God immediately presented Saul with an opportunity to share his new-found faith in Jesus Christ. The Scriptures record in Acts 9:20: "And immediately he began to proclaim Jesus in the synagogues, saying, 'He is the Son of God.'"

In verse 22 we find: "But Saul kept increasing in strength and confounding the Jews who lived at Damascus by proving that this Jesus is the Christ."

Adversity led to quality growth, which led to preparedness, which led to opportunity, which led to quantity growth.

Let me give you another example: David. In his younger years he was attacked by a lion and a bear at different times while protecting his father's sheep. God taught him how to defeat these animals and rescued him from them. Through the adversities of these attacks, he grew in his fighting skill and in his confidence in himself and, more important, in the Lord.

Finally, he was prepared. He went to fight Goliath when no one else would. This led to one of the most renowned military victories in all of history. Why? Because David had been prepared to receive God's opportunity.

PRACTICE

In light of the perspective of Gods's constructive adversity process, what exactly should we do or think? How can this help us experience joy during adversity?

First, *we should expect adversity.*

Remember 1 Peter 4:12? "Beloved, do not be surprised at the fiery ordeal among you, which comes upon you for your testing, as though some strange thing were happening to you."

In other words, don't consider it strange when you have adversity. Consider it normal. Assume that it is the beginning of something very, very significant from the Lord.

A good friend of mine recently was sharing a number of the struggles he was facing. He had personal financial difficulty; a number of investments he had participated in had gone bad simultaneously. At the same time, he had been giving considerably in support of a ministry in anticipation of other giving. Much of that other giving had not materialized, and he found himself unable to receive back much of the money he had loaned.

For various reasons, he was experiencing some snags in his jobs. He was giving serious thought as to what would be the right future direction for his life. His wife gave birth to a child in the middle of this.

This particular child had severe colic and was un-usually demanding on his wife as a result. So although she had always been a great encouragement to him, she was less available at that time.

As we were talking through all the different things he was facing, I remember saying to him, "God must be preparing you for something very, very big."

Second, *we are to be joyful when adversity comes.*

Remember James 1:2? "Consider it all joy, my brethren, when you encounter various trials."

Not only should you not be surprised at adversity but you also should, instead, be full of joy — not frustrated, and discouraged. How can you think that way? Because God is in control and He is working a wonderful long-term plan for you. The pain you experience now will be replaced by great joy when you finally see God's result (now or in heaven).

It's a little like childbirth for the mother. There is great pain for a while — according to my wife, it seems like an eternity. But when the child is born there is great joy. The pain pales in comparison to the outcome.

Third, *look for specific ways to grow from the trials.*

As we learned in the chapter about anxiety, a good method of displacing concerns is to get busy doing something. You know God wants you to grow. Cooperate with Him. Ask Him for special wisdom: "But if any of you lacks wisdom, let him ask of God, who gives to all men generously and without re-proach, and it will be given to him" (James 1:5).

Ask some mature Christian who knows you well to suggest how you might improve and grow as a result of your adversity. Take the time, effort and creativity to grow to the maximum from this event.

* * *

As a final graphic picture of how we ought to react to adversity, let me recount a scene from a 1950 movie, "Cyrano de Bergerac."

As the story goes, Cyrano was a great swords-man and a great critic of wickedness among govern-ment officials. As a result, he was not particularly popular with the leaders in his country. Because of his great courage and skill in fighting, however, they had not thought of any gentlemanly way to dispense with him.

One night in a very underhanded fashion, they arranged to have him run down by a cart. He didn't die right away. Instead, he was able with great effort, to make it to his regular appointment with the wom-an he had loved all his life and yet had never been able to marry. When she saw he was injured, she held him in her arms. Through a specific circumstance, she realized that he was the one she truly loved and now he was dying.

Despite the tenderness of that moment, as Cyrano saw death approaching, he leapt up and drew his sword. He looked death in the face. He apparent-ly "saw" various temptations and adversities from his life approaching him. He proceeded to lunge and thrust and strike out at them until he finally died.

That's a great picture of how we ought to face adversities — with anticipation and excitement and with an unwillingness to be defeated by them.

SEEING <u>YOUR</u> ADVERSITY AS GOD'S OPPORTUNITY

How are you doing? Are you excited or defeated by adversity? If defeated, review the ideas in this chapter and start applying one of them. Look forward to a day when you can "consider it all joy."

Know Where the Power Comes From

This is the most important chapter in this book. Unless you apply the biblical truths contained here, you will not succeed in the areas previously mentioned. It is not enough to know *how* to change your prayer life or Bible study, or how to handle anxiety and adversity. You also must have the *power* to do it.

Let me share with you two conversations I've had which illustrate the need for spiritual power.

While witnessing for Christ with another staff member of Campus Crusade, I ran into Ken on campus at Long Beach State University. When Ken and I completed reading through the gospel (presented in "The Four Spiritual Laws" booklet), he identified himself as a Christian who was not walking with the Lord.

At that point I explained to him what I will be sharing with you in this chapter. As I got to the point in the presentation where the attitudes and actions of the carnal (nonspiritual) Christian are described, I listed jealousy, guilt, worry, discouragement, critical spirit and frustration.

"That's me," Ken said, "that's me!"

He responded eagerly when I showed him how he could get out of his carnal state.

On another occasion I was flying from Ontario, California, to Chicago. The woman sitting across the aisle from me turned out to be from my hometown, Rockford, Illinois. We struck up an enthusiastic conversation about people and places we both knew.

In the course of the conversation she mentioned that she had gone through a divorce recently, leaving her with several children to raise.

"Joanne," I said, "I've never gone through a divorce, but I have had other experiences which have caused me great pain. Would you be interested in how I was able to be at peace in spite of those things?"

"Oh, yes!" she said.

I then explained to her what you will read in this chapter and she readily responded. We prayed together across the aisle of the plane.

OUR NEED FOR SUPERNATURAL POWER

You see God wants all of us to have a life characterized by the supernatural: supernatural joy and supernatural peace, and so much more. I know from personal contact with Christians, and from my ministry experience in a Christian organization that touches the lives of millions of people, that too few Christians are experiencing a truly abundant life. Many of them lack love, peace and contentment. They are worried, discouraged, frustrated and aimless, and they have little joy in their relationship with God. What's more, they see no way to change things.

Maybe you can relate to the problem written of by the apostle Paul in Romans 7:18*b*-20 (TLB):

> No matter which way I turn I can't make myself do right. I want to but I can't. When I want to do good, I don't; and when I try not to do wrong, I do it anyway.

That is what happens when we try to live the Christian life, which is a supernatural life, without a supernatural source of power.

In the next chapter of Romans, Paul explains that people were never intended to live the Christian life in their own natural strength. Even the strongest and best-intentioned among us will eventually fail.

If that's true, then what does God expect us to do? Here's the answer: He wants us to let Him live the Christian life in and through us.

This means that God's Spirit, the Holy Spirit, supplies everything we need to live the Christian life successfully. He has supernatural power, and He is always available.

The key to a joyful walk with God—the absolute necessity—is the Holy Spirit.

Dr. Curtis Mitchell, a professor at Biola University, tells of a job he had in his younger days at a manufacturing plant. On his first day, all day long, he lifted and stacked heavy metal castings. Hour after hour he wrestled with these big pieces of metal until by the end of the day he was so sore and tired he felt his back would break if he tried to lift one more.

About then his supervisor walked up, pointed to something over Curtis's head and asked, "Why didn't you use the hoist?"

It was never intended that he do all that work by himself. There was help available, within reach, just over his head.

So it is in the Christian life; we were never intended to live it in our own strength. Help is available—within our reach—in fact, it is within us.

The magnitude of the power of the Holy Spirit to work within us is described in Ephesians 3:16,20:

> That He would grant you, according to the riches of His glory, to be strengthened with power through His Spirit in the inner man . . . Now to Him who is able to do exceeding abundantly beyond all that we ask or think, according to the power that works within us.

First, note that one of the purposes of the Holy Spirit is to strengthen us with His power.

Second, note how great that power is: "able to do exceeding abundantly beyond all that we ask or think." A more literal translation from the Greek would read: "able to do above and beyond that which is *above and beyond* that which is **above and be-**

yond measure."

Now that is *some* power, wouldn't you say? And where does the Holy Spirit reside and work? *Within us.*

"Well," you say, "how can I appropriate that kind of power in my walk with God? It certainly would be more effective and enjoyable than what I am experiencing now!"

The following explains how. It is based on various materials on this subject written by Dr. Bill Bright (e.g., the Holy Spirit booklet, "Have You Made the Wonderful Discovery of the Spirit-Filled Life?" Campus Crusade for Christ, Inc., © 1966).

In 1 Corinthians 2:15 — 3:3 we learn that a Christian can be in one of two states, spiritual or carnal (fleshly):

> But he that is spiritual judgeth all things, yet he himself is judged of no man. For who hath known the mind of the Lord, that he may instruct him? But we have the mind of Christ. And, I, brethren, could not speak unto you as unto spiritual, but as unto carnal, even as unto babes in Christ. I have fed you with milk, and not with meat: for hitherto ye were not able to bear it, neither yet now are ye able. For ye are yet carnal: for whereas there is among you envying, and strife, and divisions, are ye not carnal, and walk as men? (KJV).

The carnal and spiritual states can be illustrated by two circles:

These circles represent the lives of the two types of Christians. Each person has received Christ, as indicated by the cross inside each circle. The spiritual Christian has put Christ *(†)* on the throne of his life; that is to say, he is allowing Christ to run his life as he is directed and empowered by the Holy Spirit.

The carnal Christian has placed self *(S)* on the throne of his life. He is running his life by himself without the benefit of God's direction and power.

Notice that in the life of the spiritual Christian, the activities, as represented by the dots, are in balance. This represents the peace, joy and purpose enjoyed by a person in harmony with God's plan and power. The interests of the carnal Christian are in disarray, representing the discord and frustration resulting from not being in harmony with God's plan or power.

A spiritual Christian is Christ-centered and empowered by the Holy Spirit. He has an effective prayer life, understands God's Word, and applies it to his life. He increasingly exhibits the fruit of the

Spirit in his life as he matures and trusts Christ to develop those qualities. That fruit, as recorded in Galatians 5:22,23, is love, joy, peace, patience, kindness, goodness, faithfulness, gentleness and self-control.

The carnal Christian's life is often characterized by unbelief, disobedience, a poor prayer life, an up-and-down spiritual experience and frustration.

God wants us all to be filled with His Spirit. In fact, He commands that we be filled. Ephesians 5:18 says: "Be filled with the Spirit." His will is clear.

Which of the two circles best represents your life? If you relate more closely to the circle on the left, and yet you sincerely desire a Spirit-filled life, you can take action now. If you truly desire to be empowered by God's Holy Spirit, you can talk to God in prayer and tell Him.

One of Scripture's most wonderful promises is found in 1 John 5:14,15. It says that if we pray and ask anything of God according to His will, He will hear and answer our prayers. It is obviously God's will that we be filled with His Spirit. After all, He commanded us to be filled. So we can know that, if we ask God to empower us with His Spirit, He will.

Why not take a few moments right now to pray? Confess to God any known sins in your life. "If we confess our sins, He is faithful and righteous to forgive us our sins and to cleanse us from all unrighteousness" (1 John 1:9). Any unconfessed sin you may have will short-circuit the flow of God's power in your life. Ask Christ to take control of the throne of your

life. Ask Him to fill you with the Holy Spirit according to His command and promise in Scripture. Finally, as an expression of your faith in Him and His
Word, thank Him for filling you.

You might not feel any different after you
pray, but as you go about the business of living each
day, trust God to empower and control you. Soon you
will begin to see the results of His power.

IF YOU SIN AGAIN

You may wonder, *If Christ is now on the throne
of my life and I'm controlled and empowered by His
Spirit, will I ever sin again? Will I ever fail God?*

Well, the answer is: likely yes, unfortunately.
Even though you have yielded the control of your life
to Christ, your ego is still very much alive. In other
words, you still have freedom of choice. You can
choose to live in your own power any time you like.

In the original Greek, the verb that is used in
Ephesians 5:18 implies "be constantly or continually
filled." Being filled with God's Spirit is not a one-
time-only occurrence. Whenever you remove Christ
from the throne, you need to restore Him to His right-
ful place in your life. When you sin, confess the sin,
and turn from it. Remove yourself from the throne of
your life and put Christ back on it.

This process could be called "spiritual breathing." When you breathe physically, you exhale the impure air and then inhale the pure. When you breathe
spiritually, you "exhale" your impure sins by confess-
ing them and you "inhale" God's pure power by ap-
propriating again the power of the Holy Spirit.

This is an ongoing process, one to be repeated whenever sin occurs in your life. The more mature Christian may need to breathe spiritually only occasionally. The newer Christian may find that he must repeat the process often. If any Christian steadily seeks to be Spirit-filled, God will be free to work in his life for good, bringing him to maturity.

As you breathe spiritually and apply the hints I've shared in other chapters, you will see your Christian life become a more joyful, exciting walk with God.

Let me go back to Galatians 5:22, to reiterate a very, very important fact. Remember what the parts of the fruit of the Spirit include? First love, and then what? Joy.

I've shared several breakthrough ideas with you in this book to help you enjoy your walk with God, but frankly, they all take a back seat to this: Be filled with the Spirit.

When you allow the Holy Spirit to fill you, *the natural result will be joy.* If you let Him control and empower you, you cannot help but have joy in your life. The Holy Spirit makes all the difference in the world.

Fred saw that very quickly. We met as we were boarding a plane in Omaha. I noticed he was carrying a Bible, and I introduced myself. I asked if he were a Christian. He said yes and we started to talk. Before we had arrived at our assigned seats inside the plane, he said, "I have been a Christian just a few months now, but I have a problem."

"Oh," I said, "what's that?"

"The Christian life is a real up-and-down experience for me. Do you have any ideas on where I can find the power to live the Christian life?"

I told Fred I had a booklet to show him that he would think was written just for him. He abandoned his assigned aisle seat and sat in the middle seat next to me so he could hear about it.

Slowly and carefully Fred and I read through the booklet on the Holy Spirit mentioned earlier. He read the Scripture passages out of his Bible. We discussed several points at some length.

Before our plane landed in Denver, Fred and I prayed. He confessed his sins and asked God's Spirit to fill him and supply the power he needed to live the Christian life with joy and victory.

BEING SURE YOU ARE FILLED

How about you? Is the Christian life an up-and-down experience for you? As you read the earlier chapters of this book, maybe you said, "Yes, but how will I be able to do that?"

If so, and you didn't pray to be filled earlier in this chapter, let me invite you to turn to appendix A at the end of this book and read through the reprint of the Holy Spirit booklet. When you get to the suggested prayer, do pray, confess your sins, and ask God to fill you with His Holy Spirit.

Then you will have the power to enjoy your walk with God.

Spread the Joy

The young man in front of me looked utterly hopeless. He sat alone on his towel at Daytona Beach, Florida, oblivious to the thousands of other people around him. His shoulders slumped forward; his knees were drawn under his chin; his eyes looked down. The time was the early '70s, around the close of the Vietnam war. He had recently come home from a tour of duty there.

"I killed a man one time with my bare hands," he told me. "Snuffed out his life. Saw his eyes bulge out and felt his body collapse." He was devastated by the experience. "I feel so guilty."

"I have good news for you," I began, and I went on to share with him how he could know Christ and experience the forgiveness He offered. At first, the young man couldn't believe it. I suppose to him it sounded too good to be true, but eventually he prayed and asked Jesus Christ into his life.

What happened in the few moments thereafter was the most dramatic metamorphosis I have ever seen. In a matter of minutes, his shoulders drew back. His countenance lifted. A smile stretched across his face from ear to ear. The joy of the Lord beamed out from his face.

He jumped to his feet with enthusiasm as we walked down the beach, discussing the decision he had made.

It reminded me of the response of the lame beggar at the temple gate:

> But Peter said, "I do not possess silver and gold, but what I do have I give to you: In the name of Jesus Christ the Nazarene—walk!" And seizing him by the right hand, he raised him up; and immediately his feet and his ankles were strengthened. And with a leap, he stood upright and began to walk; and he entered the temple with them, walking and leaping and praising God (Acts 3:6-8).

What a tremendous privilege it is when God uses us to bring His life-changing power and joy to others. If you could, wouldn't you like to do that? Wouldn't it give you joy to help give others the joy of a close fellowship with God?

The apostle John thought so.

> What was from the beginning, what we have heard, what we have seen with our eyes, what we beheld and our hands handled, concerning the Word of Life—and the life was manifested,

and we have seen and bear witness and proclaim to you the eternal life, which was with the Father and was manifested to us — what we have seen and heard we proclaim to you also, that you also may have fellowship with us; and indeed our fellowship is with the Father, and with His Son Jesus Christ. And these things we write, so that our joy may be made complete (1 John 1:1-4).

PERSPECTIVE

Certainly the scriptural command to witness is clear. Christ came to seek and to save the lost. He left us with the Great Commission:

Go therefore and make disciples of all the nations, baptizing them in the name of the Father and the Son and the Holy Spirit, teaching them to observe all that I commanded you; and lo, I am with you always, even to the end of the age (Matthew 28:19,20).

The most significant thing we can do for another is to introduce him to Christ. So why don't we do it?

- "I'm not qualified." I call this the "I am not a Billy Graham" syndrome. It is a belief that it takes years of study, training and experience to be able to introduce someone to Christ.

- "I don't want to offend anyone." We have learned there are two things we don't talk about in polite conversations — religion and politics.

- "I'm afraid of being rejected." Usually we

don't say this up front, but it's in our minds. We worry about what others will think of us, that we may be tagged as religious fanatics.

The trouble is that, when we take seriously the clear command of the Scripture that we witness, and then add to it our lack of witness, we end up with guilt. And that means we don't enjoy our walk with God.

I don't want to make the picture any darker, but I must be honest. We face another problem when we are not witnessing: When we have a lot of input into our Christian lives (from Bible study, teaching, etc.) and no output, we get spiritually stagnant. A lake that has no outlet becomes a lifeless body of water. So it is with us, and we lose our joy.

When I learned how to be filled with the Holy Spirit, as we talked about in the last chapter, God began to rescue me from all this. I saw how He could empower me to trust and obey Him—to enjoy my walk with Him.

Now let's look at another purpose of the Holy Spirit in our lives. Just before Jesus ascended into heaven, He told His disciples:

> You shall receive power when the Holy Spirit has come upon you; and you shall be my witnesses both in Jerusalem, and in all Judea and Samaria, and even to the remotest part of the earth (Acts 1:8).

So the Holy Spirit not only empowers us to live the Christian life, but He also empowers us to share it with others.

Remember Ephesians 3:20? How much power is available to help us witness? Power which is above and beyond that which is *above and beyond* that which is **above and beyond** measure. That should take care of our fears, shouldn't it?

Yet for many Christians it doesn't seem to. Why? Because they do not relate what they *have* to what they are to *share*.

SHARING WHAT YOU HAVE

Dave Foster, a very good friend of mine, once made a statement to me that beautifully summarized this thought. He said, "Witnessing is simply bearing witness to what you have."

Share what you have. That is the perspective on witnessing that moves it from the impossible to the normal.

What do I mean by "share what you have"? Well, let me give you an analogy, and then I'll explain.

Several years ago, I attended the fourth game of the World Series between the New York Yankees and the Los Angeles Dodgers. The Dodgers were behind in the series, 2 games to 1. They were in Dodger Stadium for the fourth game. Bob Welch, a fast-ball pitcher, was pitching for the Dodgers. The Yankees were good fast-ball hitters, and they proved it in the first inning. Welch gave up several runs before there was even one out. The Yankees were ahead by a number of runs before the Dodgers ever scored. It looked pretty grim.

Slowly but surely, though, the Dodgers scored

more runs and eventually moved ahead. By the top half of the ninth inning, with two outs, there had been 25 hits, 15 runs and 10 different pitchers between teams. It was an incredible game!

The Yankees trailed 8-7, but had a man on second, all ready. Then their batter hit a long, powerful fly ball up over center field. The collective heart of the Dodger fans sank. If this is a home run, the Yankees go ahead in the ninth inning. If the Yankees go on to win, they hold a 3-1 advantage in games, which would seem an insurmountable lead.

The Dodger outfielder went back, back, back ... to the warning track ... to the wall ... and he *caught* the ball! It was the final out—the Dodgers won!

The crowd, including me, went wild! I had to sit down and rest for five minutes before I had the energy to walk to my car afterward.

You know what? I've never been trained as a sportscaster, but I didn't have any trouble telling you that story. I can tell it easily and naturally. Why? Because I am a Dodger fan and that experience is something I have. I am simply sharing what I have.

So it is with witnessing—simply sharing what we have in Christ. That was true for Peter and John: "We cannot stop speaking what we have seen and heard" (Acts 4:20).

What have you seen Jesus do in your life? What have you heard or read about Him? Those are the things you have to share. Certainly, training and study will help you tremendously in your witness for

Christ, but they aren't prerequisites. Talking about Christ can be as natural as talking about baseball, or anything else that interests you. You are just sharing what you have and know personally.

You may be saying, "Right now, I don't have much I can talk about in terms of my personal walk with God. It's been kind of stale. That's why I'm reading this book."

I see your point. It is much more difficult to be enthusiastic in promoting to others what hasn't been working for you. In order to endorse to others a relationship with God, yours must be vital and satisfying.

Yet that is exactly what we have been learning about in this book—how to experience vitality and satisfaction in our walk with God. Look forward to the fact that, very soon, you will be able to share what you have.

FOR THE OTHER PERSON'S GOOD

Now let me give you another perspective to help you spread the joy of Christ more naturally. You share the gospel *for the other person's good.*

Who ultimately benefits the most from your witnessing? You? No. The people you witness to? Yes, if they respond positively.

They are the ones receiving love, joy, peace and power to cope, and eternal life besides. Yes, there are costs. For example, they will need to turn from their sins—some of which may currently be very enjoyable. Thinking people, though, who carefully examine the pros and cons of receiving Christ, will normally admit that the benefits far outweigh the costs.

In other words, you are offering them a very good deal. It is an offer they shouldn't refuse. And if you believe that, it will show as you witness. If it shows, they will get the point.

It may take a little while for them to get over their suspicion, but that can be true when any good deal is offered.

Once I was flying home from a ministry trip and, because of bad weather, I missed my connecting flight. The airline filled its obligation to get me home by giving me a ticket for another flight. Because the coach class was sold out, they gave me a first-class ticket at no extra charge.

That sounds great, doesn't it? Unless you are in full-time Christian ministry. What if some Campus Crusade supporter who knows me saw where I was sitting? What if he didn't ask about the circumstances but just assumed I had paid the extra fare? That would not be so good.

So I developed a plan. I surveyed the coach section of the plane, picked out the seat I wanted and approached the gentleman in that seat.

"Sir," I said, "I have an offer to make to you. I have in my hand a first-class boarding pass, seat 2C. Because I am discouraged by my company from flying first class, I wonder if you would trade seats with me?"

He looked at me incredulously. I'm sure he

was thinking, "Is this for real?" But after about five seconds he picked up his briefcase and moved to the front of the plane. Later he came back, smiled and said. "Thanks, I really appreciate this."

He wasn't offended one bit. My offer was for his good, and it wasn't all that hard for me to convince him.

So it is with witnessing. Once people see that the gospel really is *good* news, they tend to respond positively, and they certainly don't reject you or think ill of you for offering it to them. They will enjoy a walk with God, and so will you.

PRACTICE

How can we put these two perspectives into practice? As we meet and talk to people, how can we turn the conversation to "sharing what we have" in Christ? How can we clearly show them that receiving Jesus Christ is "for their good"?

Let me offer you three simple steps to accomplish that:

1. Ask questions.

2. Look for common ground and the "cracks."

3. Share from your experience.

First, ask rather than tell. Communication about anything is difficult if you don't know much about your audience. Be a bit of a cub reporter with them. Ask what they do, where they are from, what hobbies they have, etc.

Listen attentively. Pursue areas of obvious interest to them.

Second, what are you looking for? For one thing, you are looking for common ground, points of common interest or experience. That builds rapport quickly.

I sat down in the seat next to a fifty-year-old gentleman on a plane from Los Angeles to New York. Before we took off I found out that he was a professor in electrical engineering. I have a bachelor of science in electrical engineering. What a natural rapport builder that was.

For another thing, you are looking for the "cracks" in people's lives. Where do they have perceived needs? I'm not talking about surface needs here. What are their deep, unmet needs?

You don't have to be a psychologist to figure some of that out. For example, I find most people are experiencing pressures and anxieties of various sorts. When I speak to college students on the subject "How to Get Better Grades and Have More Fun," I ask the audience, "How many of you have exams this term?" Virtually everyone raises his or her hand.

Then I ask, "How many of you enjoy exams?" Almost no one responds positively.

Then I say, "That's a source of pressure, isn't it?" They nod yes.

Next, I list a few other sources of anxiety most of them are experiencing. And in just a few minutes they seem very interested in what I might tell them about how to experience peace in spite of pressure. Lack of peace is a crack in their lives through which the gospel can pour into their hearts.

That leads me to the **third** and last point: Share from your experience. For example, if the crack is a lack of peace, tell how God has given you peace through your relationship with Him.

That's what I talk about with the students—how Christ has given me peace that surpasses human comprehension. I tell them about receiving much-needed peace from God after blowing that first exam at Harvard Business School.

After explaining the way my relationship with God is relevant to a crack in my life as a student, I make a transition to the gospel by saying, "Many of you probably are asking how I established that kind of a relationship with God."

It was at that point of the "Grades" talk to more than two hundred students at Indiana University that a Christian friend of mine sitting at the back of the room was a bit skeptical. He seemed to be thinking, "I doubt very many are asking that question."

I went on, "There are four simple principles that explain how I established that kind of a relationship with God and how you can as well. The first is 'God loves you.' "

A hundred pencils lifted from the desks and wrote: "God loves you." My friend at the back of the room just about flipped out of his chair. He mouthed the words, "They're writing down the gospel!"

I went on to explain the "Four Spiritual Laws," which told the students more about their sin, Christ's death for their sins, His offer of forgiveness and eternal life—and peace.

That night many students indicated decisions to receive Christ. I was able to "share what I had for their good" and it made sense to them. By God's grace and through the power of the Holy Spirit drawing them, many of those students said yes to Christ.

WHY DON'T YOU TRY THIS?

You can share what you have for their good, too. Whom do you know who is at a point of deep need? Has Christ helped you in that area of your life? If so, tell that person about it. If you know how, present the gospel to them as they demonstrate interest. If you don't know how yet, bring someone with you who does. Better yet, become trained in how to present the gospel yourself.[1]

You will put them in touch with the ultimate Source of joy. And in the process, you will experience deep joy as well.

---

1   The simple presentation of the gospel I use most often is "Have You Heard of the Four Spiritual Laws?" Appendix B contains an adaptation of this booklet. These booklets are available at your local Christian bookstore.
    If you want more information on training in personal evangelism, contact a local representative of Campus Crusade for Christ, or obtain a copy of *Witnessing Without Fear* by Bill Bright, also available at your local Christian bookstore.

Start Simply and Soon

The story is told of a Christian who put a "Honk if you love Jesus" bumper sticker on the rear bumper of his car. On one particularly bad day he was driving home from work in a real stew. Needless to say, he wasn't thinking about his bumper sticker.

As he pulled up to a red stoplight, another Christian drove up behind his car, saw the bumper sticker and honked. The first man ignored him, so the second honked again . . . and again — with a big smile on his face.

The first man was getting angry about someone honking at him. One more honk was the last straw. He threw open his car door and rushed over to the other car.

The second man rolled down his window to say

"hi" and the first man punched him in the nose!

I imagine you've had days when you felt like that. Maybe you reacted angrily to one of your children. More than one mother has said, "I could have strangled her." More than one employee has said, "I felt like going right up to the boss and telling him off."

The unenjoyable parts of life don't always involve anger. Sometimes we are worried or discouraged or lonely or feeling insignificant. Those feelings happen easily in response to adverse circumstances, and sometimes even without provocation.

It's natural to feel that way, but it's not necessary that we stay that way. Jesus said:

> I came that they might have life, and might have it abundantly (John 10:10*b*).

> Come to Me, all who are weary and heavy-laden, and I will give you rest. Take My yoke upon you and learn from Me, for I am gentle and humble in heart; and YOU SHALL FIND REST FOR YOUR SOULS. For My yoke is easy, and My load is light (Matthew 11:28-30).

God really does have a wonderful plan for our lives as Christians. He wants us to enjoy our walk with Him. He doesn't intend for us to be under a gloom cloud or in other ways without the resources to live life.

WHAT WE HAVE LEARNED

So, why don't we enjoy our walk with God? Why does the Christian life turn stale, dull and irrelevant for so many people.

One significant reason is that we don't know how a Christian walk can relate to daily life. And that is what this book has been all about—showing you how to walk with God in a way that solves problems and brings vitality and joy.

First, we learned two critical aspects about prayer. One was to think of God as our personal Father rather than some sort of distant force. We can talk with Him and cultivate a close relationship. The second was the opportunity and mandate we have to talk with God all the time. How to do that is the key: Let your first stop be God.

Next, we looked at a primary benefit of walking and talking with God continuously. Worry and a walk don't mix. A walk with God displaces worry as a dominant occupier of our minds.

Isn't the Bible a key part of the Christian life? It surely is—for many reasons. One key perspective is that doing what the Bible says keeps us out of a lot of trouble, trouble we would get into otherwise, and trouble avoided is joy preserved.

But what about those daily must-do activities that aren't that pleasant? You know . . . like changing dirty diapers? Well, challenging as it seemed, we actually saw some ways to learn to like what we have to do.

"Oh sure," you ask, "but what about the real big problems—the serious adversities?" We can turn them inside out emotionally if we see them as gateways to God's opportunities.

Then came the "enabling" chapter. The Holy

Spirit is the power source for enjoying our walk with God. We need to let Him fill, direct and empower our lives.

It would be a real crime to know all this and fail to share it with others, wouldn't it? In the last chapter I shared some simple perspectives and practices about witnessing for Christ. They can turn our stutters and fear into confident smiles as we learn to spread the joy.

WHERE TO START

So where do you start? Even though the concepts are proven and practical, there are more of them than can be implemented at once. So let me offer one last thought: Start simply and soon.

Take out a sheet of paper or 3" x 5" card. On it write the one perspective or practice that seems to be most helpful to you now.

Under that statement write why you think that is true. In other words, why do you think this will work for you and benefit you?

Finally, write down how and when you will implement this in your life.

Let me give you a few examples. Suppose you are a homemaker and have some chores you don't like. Perhaps you would choose the chapter on learning to like what you have to do. To be specific, let's say you need to "remember why" more. How can you do that? Well, how about writing the reasons you do the chores on a piece of paper and keeping that paper in front of you by the kitchen sink. Maybe you would rather put up a picture portraying the benefit.

Or perhaps you work at a desk with a phone that rings off the hook. You find you don't even think about God all day long in light of the mayhem. You read about the need for continuity walk and are sure that would help your walk with God. But how can you acquire it? Well, what about letting each phone call be a cause for you to pray briefly? In the time between the first ring and when you actually pick up the receiver, thank God for something specific, or ask Him for your need at that moment, or just praise Him.

Maybe you are a truck driver. Say you want to apply the chapter on the Bible. How can you? What about buying the New Testament on cassette tapes and listening to them on your next trip? When do you think you can stop by a Christian bookstore to buy the tapes?

In summary, no matter what your circumstances, one of the best ways to get started is to write down a simple plan: What? Why? How? When?

Once you have your idea on paper, put the paper up someplace where you can see it every morning. When you notice the idea each day, pray and ask God to give you the motivation and discipline to implement it.

When that simple plan becomes a habit or is completed, select another concept on how to enjoy your walk with God more. Do another plan. Put it up. Pray and follow through.

When is a good time to start? How about now?

If you haven't taken the opportunity to pull out your sheet of paper and answer those questions yet, I encourage you to do so.

Once your simple plan is up, see if you can do one thing yet today to start implementing it. If you don't start soon, you may never start.

If you are the homemaker above, start writing the reasons or finding the picture.

If you have the office job, start your brief prayer practice the next time the phone rings at home or wherever you are.

If you are the truck driver, call a Christian bookstore and see if they have the New Testament on tape and how much it costs.

Start simply, and start soon.

One more thing: Don't forget where your power comes from. Keep praying and asking God for the power to form a new habit. Realize that you will encounter barriers. Expect that the God who offers a close relationship will empower you.

Then relax and enjoy your walk with God.

That's what my good friend, Dr. Bill Bright does. He walks more closely with God than anyone else I know. Several years ago his dad died. Bill loved his dad dearly.

Shortly after Bill heard about his dad's death, I called him to see how he was doing.

His words first shocked, then inspired me: "I am thanking God."

Thanking God! For the death of a beloved dad?

Slowly it dawned on me. He was just applying some of the same things we have been talking about. He knew God was a loving Father who allows adversity for his growth. He was praying about all things and at all times, knowing that a walk with God displaces anxiety.

He has learned to enjoy his walk with God whatever his everyday circumstances are.

And so can you.

Have You Made the Wonderful Discovery of the Spirit-Filled Life?

You may obtain copies of the Campus Crusade for Christ booklet from which this adaptation has been taken at Christian bookstores or from the publisher.

EVERY DAY CAN BE AN EXCITING ADVENTURE FOR THE CHRISTIAN who knows the reality of being filled with the Holy Spirit and who lives constantly, moment by moment, under His gracious direction.

The Bible tells us that there are three kinds of people:

1. NATURAL MAN

(One who has not received Christ)

"But a natural man does not accept the things of the Spirit of God; for they are foolishness to him, and he cannot understand them, because they are spiritually appraised" (1 Corinthians 2:14).

SELF-DIRECTED LIFE

S - Ego or finite self is on the throne
† - Christ is outside the life
• - Interests are directed by self, often resulting in discord and frustration

2. SPIRITUAL MAN

(One who is directed and empowered by the Holy Spirit)

"But he who is spiritual appraises all things . . ." (1 Corinthians 2:15).

CHRIST-DIRECTED LIFE

† - Christ is in the life and on the throne
S - Self is yielding to Christ
• - Interests are directed by Christ, resulting in harmony with God's plan

3. CARNAL MAN

(One who has received Christ, but who lives in defeat because he trusts in his own efforts to live the Christian life)

"And I, brethren, could not speak to you as to spiritual men, but as to carnal men, as to babes in Christ. I gave you milk to drink, not solid food; for you were not yet able to receive it. Indeed, even now you are not yet able, for you are still carnal. For since there is jealousy and strife among you, are you not fleshly, and are you not walking like mere men?" (1 Corinthians 3:1-3).

SELF-DIRECTED LIFE

S - Self is on the throne
† - Christ dethroned and not allowed to direct the life
• - Interests are directed by self, often resulting in discord and frustration

1 GOD HAS PROVIDED FOR US AN ABUNDANT AND FRUITFUL CHRISTIAN LIFE.

Jesus said, "I came that they might have life, and might have it abundantly" (John 10:10).

"I am the vine, you are the branches; he who abides in Me, and I in him, he bears much fruit; for apart from Me you can do nothing" (John 15:5).

"But the fruit of the Spirit is love, joy, peace, patience, kindness, goodness, faithfulness, gentleness, self-control; against such things there is no law" (Galatians 5:22,23).

"But you shall receive power when the Holy Spirit has come upon you; and you shall be My witnesses both in Jerusalem, and in all Judea and Samaria, and even to the remotest part of the earth" (Acts 1:8).

THE SPIRITUAL MAN – Some personal traits which result from trusting God:

Christ-centered
Empowered by the Holy Spirit
Introduces others to Christ
Effective prayer life
Understands God's Word
Trusts God
Obeys God
Love
Joy
Peace
Patience
Kindness
Faithfulness
Goodness

The degree to which these traits are manifested in the life depends upon the extent to which the Christian trusts the Lord with every detail of his life, and upon his maturity in Christ. One who is only beginning to understand the ministry of the Holy Spirit should not be discouraged if he is not as fruitful as more mature Christians who have known and experienced this truth for a longer period.

Why is it that most Christians are not experiencing the abundant life?

2 CARNAL CHRISTIANS CANNOT EXPERIENCE THE ABUNDANT AND FRUITFUL CHRISTIAN LIFE.

The carnal man trusts in his own efforts to live the Christian life:

A. He is either uninformed about, or has forgotten, God's love, forgiveness and power (Romans 5:8-10; Hebrews 10:1-25; 1 John 1; 2:1-3; 2 Peter 1:9; Acts 1:8).

B. He has an up-and-down spiritual experience.

C. He cannot understand himself – he wants to do what is right, but cannot.

D. He fails to draw upon the power of the Holy Spirit to live the Christian life (1 Corinthians 3:1-3; Romans 7:15-24; 8:7; Galatians 5:16-18).

THE CARNAL MAN – Some or all of the following traits may characterize the Christian who does not fully trust God:

Ignorance of his spiritual heritage
Unbelief
Disobedience
Loss of love for God and for others
Poor prayer life
No desire for Bible study
Legalistic attitude
Impure thoughts
Jealousy
Guilt
Worry
Discouragement
Critical spirit
Frustration
Aimlessness

(The individual who professes to be a Christian but who continues to practice sin should realize that he may not be a Christian at all, according to 1 John 2:3; 3:6,9; Ephesians 5:5.)

The third truth gives us the only solution to this problem . . .

3 JESUS PROMISED THE ABUNDANT AND FRUITFUL LIFE AS THE RESULT OF BEING FILLED (DIRECTED AND EMPOWERED) BY THE HOLY SPIRIT.

The Spirit-filled life is the Christ-directed life by which Christ lives His life in and through us in the power of the Holy Spirit (John 15).

A. One becomes a Christian through the ministry of the Holy Spirit, according to John 3:1-8. From the moment of spiritual birth, the Christian is indwelt by the Holy Spirit at all times (John 1:12; Colossians 2:9,10; John 14:16,17).

Though all Christians are indwelt by the Holy Spirit, not all Christians are filled (directed and empowered) by the Holy Spirit on an ongoing basis.

B. The Holy Spirit is the source of the overflowing life (John 7:37-39).

C. The Holy Spirit came to glorify Christ (John 16:1-15). When one is filled with the Holy Spirit, he is a true disciple of Christ.

D. In His last command before His ascension, Christ promised the power of the Holy Spirit to enable us to be witnesses for Him (Acts 1:1-9).

How, then, can one be filled with the Holy Spirit?

4 WE ARE FILLED (DIRECTED AND EM-POWERED) BY THE HOLY SPIRIT BY FAITH; THEN WE CAN EXPERIENCE THE ABUNDANT AND FRUITFUL LIFE WHICH CHRIST PROMISED TO EACH CHRISTIAN.

You can appropriate the filling of the Holy Spirit **right now** if you:

A. Sincerely desire to be directed and empowered by the Holy Spirit (Matthew 5:6; John 7:37-39).

B. Confess your sins. By **faith** thank God that He **has** forgiven all of your sins — past, present and future — because Christ died for you (Colossians 2:13-15; 1 John 1; 2:1-3; Hebrews 10:1-17).

C. Present every area of your life to God (Romans 12:1,2).

D. By **faith** claim the fullness of the Holy Spirit, according to:

1. HIS COMMAND — Be filled with the Spirit. "And do not get drunk with wine, for that is dissipation, but be filled with the Spirit" (Ephesians 5:18).

2. HIS PROMISE — He will always answer when we pray according to His will. "And this is the confidence which we have before Him, that, if we ask any-

thing according to His will, He hears us. And if we know that He hears us in whatever we ask, we know that we have the requests which we have asked from Him" (1 John 5:14,15).

Faith can be expressed through prayer . . .

How to Pray in Faith to Be Filled With the Holy Spirit

We are filled with the Holy Spirit by **faith** alone. However, true prayer is one way of expressing your faith. The following is a suggested prayer:

"Dear Father, I need You. I acknowledge that I have been directing my own life and that, as a result, I have sinned against You. I thank You that You have forgiven my sins through Christ's death on the cross for me. I now invite Christ to again take His place on the throne of my life. Fill me with the Holy Spirit as You **commanded** me to be filled, and as You **promised** in Your Word that You would do if I asked in faith. I pray this in the name of Jesus. As an expression of my faith, I now thank You for directing my life and for filling me with the Holy Spirit."

Does this prayer express the desire of your heart? If so, bow in prayer and trust God to fill you with the Holy Spirit **right now.**

How to Know That You Are Filled (Directed and Empowered) by the Holy Spirit

Did you ask God to fill you with the Holy Spirit? Do you know that you are now filled with the Holy Spirit? On what authority? (On the trustworthiness of God Himself and His Word: Hebrews 11:6; Romans 14:22,23.)

Do not depend upon feelings. The promise of God's Word, not our feelings, is our authority. The Christian lives by faith (trust) in the trustworthiness of God Himself and His Word.

This train diagram illustrates the relationship between **fact** (God and His Word), **faith** (our trust in God and His Word), and **feeling** (the result of our faith and obedience) (John 14:21).

The train will run with or without the caboose. However, it would be futile to attempt to pull the train by the caboose. In the same way, we, as Christians, do not depend upon feelings or emotions, but we place our faith (trust) in the trustworthiness of God and the promises of His Word.

How to Walk in the Spirit

Faith (trust in God and in His promises) is the only means by which a Christian can live the Spirit-directed life. As you continue to trust Christ moment by moment:

A. Your life will demonstrate more and more of the fruit of the Spirit (Galatians 5:22,23) and will be more and more conformed to the image of Christ (Romans 12:2; 2 Corinthians 3:18).

B. Your prayer life and study of God's Word will become more meaningful.

C. You will experience His power in witnessing (Acts 1:8).

D. You will be prepared for spiritual conflict against the world (1 John 2:15-17); against the flesh (Galatians 5:16,17); and against Satan (1 Peter 5:7-9; Ephesians 6:10-13).

E. You will experience His power to resist temptation and sin (1 Corinthians 10:13; Philippians 4:13; Ephesians 1:19-23; 6:10; 2 Timothy 1:7; Romans 6:1-16).

Spiritual Breathing

By faith you can continue to experience God's love and forgiveness.

If you become aware of an area of your life (an attitude or an action) that is displeasing to the Lord, even though you are walking with Him and sincerely desiring to serve Him, simply thank God that He has forgiven your sins — past, present and future — on the basis of Christ's death on the cross. Claim His love and forgiveness by faith and continue to have fellowship with Him.

If you retake the throne of your life through sin — a definite act of disobedience — breathe spiritually.

Spiritual Breathing (exhaling the impure and inhaling the pure) is an exercise in faith and enables you to continue to experience God's love and forgiveness.

1. **Exhale** — confess your sin — agree with God concerning your sin and thank Him for His forgiveness of it, according to 1 John 1:9 and Hebrews 10:1-25. Confession involves repentance — a change in attitude and action.

2. **Inhale** — surrender the control of your life to Christ, and appropriate (receive) the fullness of the Holy Spirit by faith. Trust that He now directs and empowers you, according to the **command** of Ephesians 5:18 and the **promise** of 1 John 5:14,15.

* * * * *

Would You Like to Know God Personally?

The following four principles will help you discover how to know God personally and experience the abundant life He promised.

1

GOD **LOVES** YOU AND CREATED YOU TO KNOW HIM PERSONALLY.

(References contained in these pages should be read in context from the Bible whenever possible.)

God's Love

"For God so loved the world, that He gave His only begotten Son, that whoever believes in Him should not perish, but have eternal life" (John 3:16).

God's Plan

"Now this is eternal life: that they may know you, the only true God, and Jesus Christ, whom you have sent" (John 17:3, NIV).

What prevents us from knowing God personally?

2

MAN IS **SINFUL** AND **SEPARATED** FROM GOD, SO WE CANNOT KNOW HIM PERSONALLY OR EXPERIENCE HIS LOVE.

Man Is Sinful

"For all have sinned and fall short of the glory of God" (Romans 3:23).

Man was created to have fellowship with God; but, because of his stubborn self-will, he chose to go his own independent way, and fellowship with God was broken. This self-will, characterized by an attitude of active rebellion or passive indifference, is evidence of what the Bible calls sin.

Man Is Separated

"For the wages of sin is death" (spiritual separation from God) (Romans 6:23).

This diagram illustrates that God is holy and man is sinful. A great gulf separates the two. The arrows illustrate that man is continually trying to reach God and establish a personal relationship with Him through his own efforts, such as a good life, philosophy or religion.

The third principle explains the only way to bridge this gulf . . . .

3 JESUS CHRIST IS GOD'S **ONLY** PROVISION FOR MAN'S SIN. THROUGH HIM ALONE WE CAN KNOW GOD PERSONALLY AND EXPERIENCE HIS LOVE.

He Died in Our Place

"But God demonstrates His own love toward us, in that while we were yet sinners, Christ died for us" (Romans 5:8).

He Rose From the Dead

"Christ died for our sins . . . He was buried . . . He was raised on the third day, according to the Scriptures . . . He appeared to Peter, then to the twelve. After that He appeared to more than five hundred" (1 Corinthians 15:3-6).

He Is the Only Way to God

"Jesus said to him, 'I am the way, and the truth, and the life; no one comes to the Father, but through Me' " (John 14:6).

This diagram illustrates that God has bridged the gulf which separates us from Him by sending His Son, Jesus Christ, to die on the cross in our place to pay the penalty for our sins.

GOD / JESUS / MAN

It is not enough just to know these truths . . .

4 WE MUST INDIVIDUALLY **RECEIVE** JESUS CHRIST AS SAVIOR AND LORD; THEN WE CAN KNOW GOD PERSONALLY AND EXPERIENCE HIS LOVE.

We Must Receive Christ

"But as many as received Him, to them He gave the right to become children of God, even to those who believe in His name" (John 1:12).

We Receive Christ Through Faith

"For by grace you have been saved through faith; and that not of yourselves, it is the gift of God; not as a result of works, that no one should boast" (Ephesians 2:8,9).

When We Receive Christ, We Experience a New Birth. (Read John 3:1-8.)

We Receive Christ by Personal Invitation

(Christ is speaking): "Behold, I stand at the door and knock; if anyone hears My voice and opens the door, I will come in to him" (Revelation 3:20).

Receiving Christ involves turning to God from self (repentance) and trusting Christ to come into our lives to forgive our sins and to make us the kind of people He wants us to be. Just to agree intellectually that Jesus Christ is the Son of God and that He died on the cross for our sins is not enough. Nor is it enough to have an emotional experience. We receive Jesus Christ by faith, as an act of the will.

These two circles represent two kinds of lives:

SELF-DIRECTED LIFE
S – Self is on the throne
† – Christ is outside the life
● – Interests are directed by self, often resulting in discord and frustration

CHRIST-DIRECTED LIFE
† – Christ is in the life and on the throne
S – Self is yielding to Christ
● – Interests are directed by Christ, resulting in harmony with God's plan

Which circle best represents your life? Which circle would you like to have represent your life?

The following explains how you can invite Jesus Christ into your life·